BOB PIERCE
This One Thing I Do

BOB PIERCE
This One Thing I Do

FRANKLIN GRAHAM
with
JEANETTE LOCKERBIE

WORD PUBLISHING
Dallas · London · Sydney · Singapore

BOB PIERCE: THIS ONE THING I DO

Copyright © 1983 by Samaritan's Purse

All rights reserved. No portion of this book may be reproduced in any form, except for brief quotations in reviews, without written permission from the publisher.

Library of Congress Cataloging in Publication Data

Graham, Franklin, 1952–
  Bob Pierce, this one thing I do.

  1. Pierce, Bob, 1914–1978.   2. Evangelists—United
States—Biography.   I. Lockerbie, Jeanette W.   II. Title.
BV3785.P53G7   1983
269'.2'0924 [B]   82–24729
ISBN 0-8499-0097-2 (hard cover)
ISBN 0-8499-3352-8 (trade paper)

Grateful appreciation to *World Vision* magazine for permission to reprint portions of the article, "Humanity's Friend," October 1978, pp. 18–23.

Scripture quotations in this publication are from the following sources:
  The King James Version of the Bible (KJV).
  The New International Version of the Bible (NIV), published by the Zondervan Corporation, copyright © 1978 by the New York International Bible Society.
  The Living Bible, Paraphrased (TLB), copyright © 1971 by Tyndale House Publishers, Wheaton, Illinois.
  The Revised Standard Version of the Bible (RSV), copyright © 1946, 1952, © 1971 and 1973 by the Division of Christian Education of the National Council of the Churches of Christ in the U.S.A.

Printed in the United States

4 5 6 7 8 9 LBM 14 13 12 11

This book is dedicated to
the family of
Dr. Robert Willard Pierce
and his wife Lorraine.

Contents

Foreword

IT WAS A MISTAKE to decide just to glance at the manuscript of this book early one Thursday morning before going to the Senate restaurant for breakfast. Mistake, because it took real discipline to stop reading. Memories exploded in my mind taking me back to 1949. Reading these pages was like traveling with Bob, and the memories were real and precious.

Some of us had been working on a plan to have Bob nominated for the Nobel Peace Prize before his death. I was convinced that no one anywhere in the world was more deserving or qualified than he. His presence and ministry among the leadership of Southeast Asia had a powerful influence for peace. He was certainly an ambassador without portfolio, commending the United States and the compassion of the American people to the neediest of the needy as well as to the affluent. He was respected, admired, loved, and sought after by the leaders of the Asian churches. His passion for Christ, and his compassion for people of all races, was like a catalyst that drew men and women together and nurtured their unity in Christ and their love for one another.

Bob Pierce belonged to the world and his great heart embraced all peoples. He prayed more earnestly and importunely than anyone else I have ever known. It was as though prayer burned within him as he sought to respond wherever there was need. He prayed for nations, churches, and persons as specifically and precisely as I pray for those in our prayer breakfast fellowship. It was as though he had a burden from which there was no relief except in intercession. Often he would awaken me during the night as he agonized in prayer, and I was persuaded that, at times, he would pray in his sleep.

Early in my walk with Christ, God laid the world on my heart: first Korea, then Latin America, then Africa, then China. Each situation provoked a struggle which was not resolved until I offered myself for mission in each of those countries. God gave me a vision for the world through college and seminary, but that vision remained academic until I met Bob Pierce. It was he that God used to make the vision a reality; and because of him, I have had the rare privilege of ministering in those lands many times through the years.

As a pastor, first in Hollywood, California, and later in Washington, D.C., I was never able to think of a local congregation in any other way than that it had an obligation to the ends of the earth. The church existed for mission to the whole world, and such thinking was as natural for me as the church's obligation to its own community, its own city. Bob Pierce discipled me to think this way by his precept and example. I can recall often experiencing sheer amazement at his capacity to bear concern for the world and all its suffering multitudes.

Reading the manuscript for this book was the nearest thing to being with Bob that I have ever experienced since Christ called him home. It was almost as if I could hear him share his experiences and concerns. One subject which seemed to occupy his thoughts continually was the heroism of many hidden-away servants of Christ whose exploits of faith were awesome. They were authentic heroes who had profound influence in his life and to whom he ministered unfailingly and relentlessly. They were unheard of and Bob often spoke of wanting to tell their story, not simply to honor them, though he felt they deserved it, but that their extraordinary labors of love might bless the whole body of Christ and serve as an example to believers. It was a source of great satisfaction that the stories of some of these courageous and faithful saints occur in this book.

Bob Pierce was truly an uncommon man, an unusual mixture of humility and ego, drive and restraint, strength and weakness, boldness and timidity, faith and doubt. As becomes clear in this volume, Bob lived every hour of his life in complete amazement that God could use him. He was not unmindful of his gifts, but he was always awed by the magnitude of the mission to which God called him. No matter how much he was able to do in how many places, it was never enough. Restless to give himself to the world, yet he never became a victim of a messianic complex. With all his "charisma" he remained a simple servant whom God used to do the impossible again and again and again.

Bob was the incarnation of love and generosity. Response to any need, however great, constituted a mandate for him. One of his biggest frustrations, as World Vision grew, was the requirement of the IRS that grants be approved by the Board before they were made. He understood this necessity but never found it easy to live with. It was virtually impossible for him not to respond to a need on the spot, however great. I recall one occasion early in the life of World Vision when Bob wrote a check for forty thousand dollars to cover a desperate need in India, then wired Frank Phillips at home urging him to cover the check. It was done. Although the amounts were not always that large, it was not unusual for him to promise a grant or write a check for which he requested Board approval at the next meeting.

Bob Pierce functioned from a broken heart. It was absolutely uncanny how he would manage to be at a place of crisis when it occurred. It was as if he absorbed tragedy in his own body and then communicated it so vividly to people, both in speaking and writing, that they could identify with it as though they were there. It took a good deal of restraint to resist a Bob Pierce appeal for the suffering.

This book is Bob Pierce in the raw—as he was and as God used him. He was a sinner—and no one knew that better than he—but he knew also the exceedingly gracious forgiveness of our Lord. He was extraordinarily gifted, but never impressed by his gifts. He was simply grateful. From Bob's standpoint, he was an earthen vessel available at all times for the exclusive use of his Lord. One of his most common prayers was, "Lord, I give you license to interfere in my life and plans at any time, in any way, at any cost to me." He was totally, unreservedly, irrevocably, committed to Christ; and two remarkable ministries, World Vision and Samaritan's Purse, witness to the effectiveness with which God used him.

I think I knew Bob Pierce as intimately as anyone except his family. It was often very difficult to be with him and I was never uncritical in our relationship; but I believe I am well within the mark when I say that he stands with the most faithful of God's servants throughout the centuries. He failed much as husband and father, and this fact as much as any human tragedy was the reason for his broken heart. His love for his wife and daughters was exceeded only by his sense of failing to be to them what he wished to be. He caused pain to many, but God used him to be a comforter beyond description to thousands.

Bob Pierce was evangelist, missionary, preacher, pastor, sociologist, humanitarian, statesman, by the grace of God and to the glory of God.

RICHARD C. HALVERSON
Chaplain of the United States Senate
Washington, D.C.

Preface

DR. BOB PIERCE WAS one of the great evangelical humanitarians of this century—motion picture producer, radio program host, author, lecturer, co-founder of Youth for Christ, founder of World Vision, and, later in his life, founder and president of Samaritan's Purse; but first, last, and always—an evangelist.

Shortly after the death of Dr. Bob, the Board of Directors asked if I would be willing to take the leadership of Samaritan's Purse and the responsibility for completing his book, which Bob had started before his death. He had taped over a hundred and fifty hours concerning a lifetime of principles and experiences. After much prayer, we felt led to contact Jeanette Lockerbie, a professional writer with years of mission experience. We finally caught up with her in Bangladesh, where she was visiting her missionary daughter, Jeannie. We needed someone who could help me wade through this mound of material left by Dr. Bob—someone who would put it in such an order that God would be given the glory, but also in such a way that would preserve the principles that had guided Bob's life. I believe Jeanette has done just that.

I narrate the chapters, but it is Jeanette who has put it all together and made this possible. It has been a privilege to have known Bob Pierce and to have had a small part in the development of these pages. I trust they will touch your heart and bless you as they have me.

FRANKLIN GRAHAM
Boone, North Carolina

*   *   *

Before his death Bob Pierce once stated, "I am writing this book like a freak; which means I interrupt my own thoughts about every third sentence. Before you find the end of the story I started, I think of so many things in between that I am led off on side trips. I don't know whether we will be able to make a book out of this or not."

Then he prayed, "It's out of my hands; it's in Your hands, God."

So why and how did it get into my hands?

I was short-terming in Asia, conducting writing workshops for Christian nationals, when a request came to me from the executive vice-president of Samaritan's Purse, Mr. George D. Johnston, that I consider collaborating with Rev. Franklin Graham on this book (Franklin having become president of Samaritan's Purse).

It did not take too much prayer, thought, and deliberation for me to make my decision. Also, my daughter, Jeannie, in Bangladesh encouraged me that—yes, this book was certainly in my area.

Dr. Bob Pierce and his work was not new to me. Long before we actually met, I had heard of him as a dynamic Youth for Christ speaker. Bob was one of the founders of YFC. His first film, *China Challenge,* had moved me so that I still remembered it. Then as the founder and president of *World Vision,* his name had become synonymous with Christlike compassion for the spiritually lost and physically suffering people of the world. I had seen and heard his wonderful Korean Orphan Choir. In one instance I had even helped with the publicity for their performance.

Later, in my travels when I ran into Bob Pierce in the Hong Kong airport, it had been like meeting an old friend. I had learned he was now the president of Samaritan's Purse, an organization he founded to carry out the intent of the parable Jesus told. As always, he was selflessly giving his all for the Cross of Christ.

I was used to seeing faces light up at the mention of his name, and to hearing of specific instances when his being there, or supplying a particularly critical item made a significant difference in a crisis situation.

In some cases, I was even a beneficiary of his compassionate concern for missionaries as, while working with them, I enjoyed some special treats he had thoughtfully provided.

So, although I realized that the project would entail months of soaking up, selecting, and digesting the mountain of transcribed material from the more than one hundred and fifty hours Bob had taped, I unhesitatingly accepted the assignment. (In the process of completing it, Franklin Graham and I spent long days and hours at Samaritan's Purse headquarters in Boone, North Carolina.)

Barely had I begun my research when I discovered another vital link, a special reason why it was *right* that I should collaborate on the Samaritan's Purse/Bob Pierce story. I learned that the young missionary to whom Bob attributed his first eye-opening that led to his personal world vision—Beth Albert, R.N.—was the same person who had been the subject of the first article I wrote for publication, A *Hundred Percent for God.* Bob had met her in Kunming, China—and his life had never been the same.

In the last few years before his death I would hear people ask someone, "Did you know that Bob Pierce is *dying of* leukemia?" and I always wanted to butt in with the answer, "No! Bob Pierce is not *dying of* leukemia; he is *living with* leukemia!" He was the first to say, "I've had some of my greatest adventures since I've 'been dying.'"

In my own area of Southern California, many are the tales people are telling me of Bob's early days; some come from his old friends who believed in him and went along with his ventures for God which called for massive faith; others—more realistic, perhaps—came from those who applauded but were more cautious and remembered, in a kindly way, the occasional fiasco.

This book presents the real Bob Pierce; for it is he himself who tells of his warts, flaws, failings, and an abundance of simple faith in a God Who lives and cares about people today. Bob especially lived for what he called the "little" people. Overriding all else, Bob Pierce was, as perhaps best expressed by Pat Robertson in an interview with Bob on the 700 Club, "a man restless to win souls."

As it has been my privilege to work on this book, I have at times almost sensed Bob's presence and heard him say, "That's it; that's what I'm trying to say."

Personally, I have been inspired, blessed beyond measure, and challenged by what God can and does do through a man who will let Him.

JEANETTE LOCKERBIE
Pasadena, California

Introduction

I FIRST MET BOB PIERCE at a hotel in Chicago where we were having a preliminary organizational meeting for Youth for Christ International. I saw this ruggedly handsome young man standing in the background. I went up to him and introduced myself, and with an infectious grin I will never forget, he said, "I am Bob Pierce from Los Angeles, and I am really interested in Youth for Christ. Is there any way that I could get to meet Torrey Johnson, the founding father of Youth for Christ International?" I said, "Certainly!" I took him and introduced him to Torrey Johnson, who gave him a great big bear hug as Torrey usually did—even with strangers whom he liked.

From that day on, Bob and I became friends.

An ardent admirer of Dawson Trotman, who founded the Navigators (an organization that emphasizes Scripture memorization), Bob used the Navigators' method of memorizing Bible verses and became excellent at winning others to Christ "one-on-one."

In the meantime, Bob had enlarged his vision to include China and Korea. The films he made on China and on Korea had a tremendous impact on Christians in America. He later became the director of Youth for Christ in Los Angeles.

During the Los Angeles Crusade in 1949 when I was running out of sermons and feeling physically rather weak, I asked Bob if he would preach for me one night. He did so with great effectiveness.

Bob also introduced me to Dick Ross who, at that time, was one of the directors of broadcasting for the Mutual Broadcasting Company, but who was much more interested in motion pictures. Dick had helped Bob in making his two films and had launched Great Commission Films.

Later, Bob told me he was going to Korea and asked me to go with him over Christmastime. His intent was to visit missionaries, and he wanted me to preach in some open-air meetings.

Little did I dream that being with Bob Pierce was to greatly enlarge my vision in world missions, and also in the use of motion pictures to proclaim the Gospel.

As you will soon find out in reading the pages of this book, in some ways Bob had a complex personality. He was a man of many moods. And even though he had one of the tenderest hearts of any man I ever knew, he could also fly off the handle if he thought that something was unjust or if he had been wronged.

One of his greatest gifts was not only the vision of a lost and hurting world (which he set about to help with every ounce of energy he had), but he also was the greatest raiser of money for missions I ever knew. He could have an audience laughing and weeping and wholeheartedly emptying their pocketbooks when the offering plate was passed!

Bob Pierce was the friend of the "little" people, the forgotten, the hurting people who are unheard of and unsung except in the courts of heaven.

He founded World Vision which has become one of the largest social and religious institutions in the world.

After he retired from World Vision, Bob's restless spirit would not allow him to stop. He founded another organization that was probably even closer to his heart at the end of his life— Samaritan's Purse.

I never dreamed of the impact Bob would have on my son Franklin's life, imparting to him the same vision that he had, and requesting through his Board that Franklin take over the leadership of his work when he was called to heaven.

Bob Pierce will always be special to me.

DR. BILLY GRAHAM
Montreat, North Carolina

Bob Pierce's Prayer and Aspiration for This Book

DR. BOB PIERCE expended himself in his last days to relive and record his years of missionary endeavor. He asked God for added time to complete this task. On his deathbed, in the presence of Franklin Graham and Dr. Pierce's secretary, he voiced this prayer for the book he envisioned:

I believe, Lord, that through this book we can glorify You without puffing up the flesh. I pray that You will overrule, that You will especially fit whoever will go through all this material and write the book, so that they will glorify Christ. Cause them, O Lord, to bleed with every need, to have the qualifications to know what a missionary project is—what missionary needs *really* are. Give them sensitive hearts, Lord, so that they may reach some other sensitive hearts who would want to care but don't know how to care. May Your Holy Spirit permeate every page of what will eventually be written, and may it genuinely affect lives. It lies beyond my hands now; I leave it in Your hands, Lord. . . .

Amen

PART ONE

Dr. Bob Pierce

1. Bob Pierce, The Man

AS THE SON OF A prominent evangelist, I've been privileged to meet many Christian leaders, but I never met another man who compared with Dr. Robert Pierce.

Nobody was neutral about him. Mention his name in certain circles even today and faces glow as people verbally tumble over each other to enthusiastically relate some unforgettable part he played in their lives. The same name can also evoke a rash of negative comments.

Such response is predictable for a man whose parish was the world of human need. The only way to assure freedom from criticism is to do nothing, make no waves, rock no boats. The most vulnerable to attack are those who, like the heroes of the ages, dare to risk all to serve the Lord Jesus Christ. Such a man was Bob Pierce.

There is no way of understanding Bob Pierce apart from a consideration of the contract he made with God a few years after he accepted Christ as his Saviour. He prayed:

Lord, I don't know how to run my life. I'm second-rate, but will you let me have a chance at doing the best a second-rater can do? And if you will help me, I promise that I won't say no. I'll sign a contract with You right now, and let the angels record it forever in heaven, that I give You a license to do Your will with me, *whether I like it or not*—irrevocable for the rest of my life. You can write in anything You want, and I can scream my head off and beg and deny it and say I want out; but I give You authority *forever* to do Your will in my life.

And he figuratively signed his name to it. In this, he joined the ranks of other men before him whose names live on in the annals of Christian missions.

"God took the actual nothing that I was," Dr. Bob would say, "and time and again He put me in the right spot at the right time to see a need that took more than I had faith to fill."

That last part is something of an understatement!

What kind of man was he, this Bob Pierce who is known around the world for his unstinting labor to help God's "little" people? (Not "little" in the eyes of God, "little" in the eyes of people). Those of us who knew him well, who worked with him, traveled with him, saw him in both sickness and health, and who appreciated him, were well aware of the contradictions of his nature.

He would have been the last to think of himself as *a humble man.* Yet his own admissions belie that. How often I've heard him say something like this:

If there's anything I can thank God for in my life, it is that I may not have had too many brains. I never was an intellectual, I was never a polished speaker, and I can remember when Mrs. Rimmer (wife of the noted Bible teacher, Dr. Harry Rimmer), who listened to my nationwide radio broadcast wrote, "Dear Dr. Bob, I love you. I love your ministry, I love your stories, but I no longer will be listening after today. Every Sunday I have listened to you mangle English grammar and I simply cannot stand to listen one more time to a man who does not know the difference between the words *lay* and *lie.* But I'll support you." And she did, but I do mangle the King's English.*

---

*Author's note: In the interest of realism, we have to some degree retained Bob's "mangled English."

Or, one day shortly before his death, when reminiscing with his long-time friends and colleagues, Larry Ward and Ellsworth Culver, he quipped:

> You're right. Everything I ever did for the Lord, all my life, proves I am not a clever man. Mostly God had to backhand me into things. Seems I was so dumb, that God could never just say to me, "Go from here to there," as He could to somebody else who would do that. But me? I had to climb over a wall or fall down a well . . . , when for the other guy it would be a fifteen-minute walk. I eventually would get there and at least I did have brains enough to say, "Well, the *Lord* got me here, not my own ability"—which the Lord seemed to enjoy, because the Bible does say, "I am the LORD . . . and my glory will I not give to another" [Isa. 42:8, KJV]. God had found out, I guess, that doing things through Bob Pierce was one sure way that the people would know that He, the Lord had done it, not me! And I'm grateful for that. If I had got my head swelled, the Lord might have lifted His hands off me. But I knew I didn't have a lot of gifts like some men have; the "gift" I had was to stumble on things, and somehow God could use that.

Dr. Bob was well aware that he couldn't do what he did alone; he readily admits, "There was never a way for anybody to do enough to meet all the need. So I just obeyed God and did as much as He gave me faith and the ability to do, and He brought others to help who were willing to obey Him."

Unorthodox describes Pierce, the man.

His methods would never find their way into a missions manual. As an eager young convert of two weeks, he won his best buddy to Christ. "And I hadn't learned any Bible verses yet;" then he would poke gentle fun at his dear friend, Dawson Trotman: "Daws would get upset at the thought that God could use somebody before he had memorized the thirty-two Navigator verses," he would quip.

Dr. Bob's unorthodox methods were often mistaken for sheer arrogance or a disdain for established ways of doing missionary work. (And at times he was indeed rebelling at the

status quo methods, which in his opinion sometimes amounted
to limiting God.)

Dr. Garth Hunt (now Canadian Director of Living Bibles
International), who met Bob first in Saigon, later said:

> In my judgment, Dr. Bob Pierce was the undisputed champion of
> the "little" people of the world. But ironically, he was also one of
> the most difficult men I ever worked with and these contradictions
> were a conundrum to many of us. You had to have opportunity to
> get to know the man before you could understand him and fully
> appreciate what he was doing or attempting to do. When I first met
> him in Vietnam, he appeared to me to have grandiose ideas of what
> *he* was going to do in Vietnam. His plans seemed to overwhelm
> me, and I wasn't sure that he needed any of the rest of us. I felt
> quite disappointed that day.
>
> Years later, I made this observation: one should not judge Bob
> Pierce on a first meeting. He was the kind of man you had to get to
> know—the real man. It was as I saw him in the hospital, watched
> how he was with the amputees, the paraplegics and others who
> were suffering horribly because of that war, that I got a glimpse of
> the heart of this man. And *never* have I seen such compassion and
> empathy manifested! *That* was the real Bob Pierce.

As Garth Hunt came to understand, there's a reason why
Dr. Bob appeared difficult to work with: he had this commitment to God and to needy people, and he was determined to
give both the best. So he could not stand mediocrity. He took
literally Revelation 3:15,16: "I know thy works, that thou are
neither cold nor hot: I would thou wert cold or hot. So then
because thou art lukewarm, and neither cold nor hot, I will
spew thee out of my mouth." Like few men I've met, Dr. Bob
could spew out of his life those who were serving God half-
heartedly. He knew where he was going—he knew what he
was going to do—and he was determined to get there.

His unorthodox ways started in childhood. As a three-year-
old, because he had learned all the verses, Bob was to sing
"Away in a Manger" at the Sunday School Christmas Concert.
He practiced his solo. Then the night of the performance, he

got up and sang the first verse, started the second, stopped—said out loud, *"That's enough,"*—and marched off the platform.

Bob's Leadership Ability

From his earliest days as a Christian, according to his beloved Sunday School teacher, Bob showed signs of being able to lead others. This teacher, Mrs. Elisabeth Sales, was also responsible for the junior young people's group, and she recalls that Bob was just twelve when they elected him president. Describing the youth group, their former teacher says they would gather at shopping centers and sing and give testimonies—even when their non-Christian schoolmates would come around and heckle them. And they spent their Sunday afternoons visiting lonely shut-ins, taking some treats to add to the older people's day. She remembers how Bob was always in the forefront of the activity and always finding more ways to express his faith. "It never surprised me that the Lord took this dedicated pupil of mine and made him such a power around the world," she said.

In later days, Bob's leadership ability bred some resentment and misunderstandings. Yet, God needs leaders to see that His work gets done. And in some instances former critics become genuine admirers. "I was prepared to overlook his domineering ways of treating some of us, when I realized what he was committed to. There was no question that Bob Pierce was a general and he was commanding all of us," one colleague admits.

To that, Larry Ward and Garth Hunt both agree. "We were sold on Bob's vision to alleviate the suffering and to share the love of Jesus Christ and the reality of a living Saviour. This is what was most important. And anyway, more often than not he was right! *He had a great sense of knowing what to do at the right time."*

Characteristic of Bob's leadership was his unwillingness to accept excuses, as those who worked with him were well aware. He never veered from: *"Don't tell me it can't be done until you have exhausted every avenue . . . then I'll accept your explanation."*

The common sense fact, I have learned, is that when we take this approach, we usually find that *it can be done.* More than one man credits Bob Pierce's insistence on this philosophy-in-action for helping them in their own service for God.

Awareness of His Faults and Failings

Unquestionably, Dr. Bob had no illusions about himself and his sometimes adverse affect on other people.

Not long before the Lord took him home, he said, "One of the hardest things I've had to endure all my life was this temperament of mine. It's kept me busy saying, 'I *know* I did it and I was wrong; I have nobody to blame but myself.' It's not easy to admit, yet I've had to do it time and time again. I'd sin, or I'd disobey God, or I'd grow careless, or I'd let the purity of my motives be polluted by my own ego—my own carnal ambition or my own desires would take over. I tell you, the hardest thing in the world is to face up to reality—acknowledge the actual facts. We are what *we* are—and the Lord is Who *He* is . . . and He says, '*I am the Lord. That is my name, and my glory will I not give to another.'* So the secret of succeeding, as Dr. Bob Cook, president of King's College, once told me, is *lasting:* it's failing, getting up and acknowledging that you failed, asking forgiveness where you need to, and getting up again and taking another stab at it."

I always appreciated this in Bob Pierce. He was keenly aware of his faults and deplored them openly. But he got up and tried again. He didn't sit around wringing his hands and moaning, "O wretched man that I am!" That can be totally debilitating (and maybe a mark of false humility); it certainly doesn't glorify God and it doesn't help anybody.

Another thing about Dr. Bob as I knew him is that he didn't slough off the blame on other people. Like when Mrs. Harry

Rimmer pointed out that he "mangled the English language." He would say, "I'm one guy who got through high school and most of four years of college without ever learning basic grammar." But then he was quick to add, "But don't blame my teachers. Bob Pierce was lookin' out the window."

Bob's Ability to Laugh at Himself

With great glee he would tell this story: "Dr. Donald Grey Barnhouse was once asked, 'Why in the world do you travel around the world with a character like Bob Pierce?'—me being an old sawdust trail type o'guy while Dr. Barnhouse was such an intellectual giant. And here's what he would reply: *'I go around the world with Bob Pierce because he's the only man who's so theologically ignorant that I can't argue with him.'*

"So Dr. Barnhouse and I had great times together. I just read what the Bible said and believed it, whether it was out of context or not. And Dr. Barnhouse taught me a little about *how to find* the context!"

Dr. Bob's sense of humor was always coming out; mostly it was at his own expense, and people loved him for it. He was so forthright.

I remember well the day he said to me, "Franklin, do you know that it was your own father [Dr. Billy Graham] who saved me from a life of fraudulent doctorhood? What I mean is this: That first time I went to Korea I was so young, and the orientals are super courteous people, so to show some respect even though I had done nothing to merit it, they 'doctored' me—and it just kind of stuck throughout those countries. Then, one day, your father legitimized me, you might say.

"At that time," he explained, "your father was President of Northwestern College, and the powers that be in that institution somehow decided that what God was allowing me to do for Him was worthy of some kind of recognition. So they called me to the convocation, handed me a citation, put a hood over my head and dubbed me Litt. D., Doctor of Letters."

Dr. Bob never tried to hide anything, or pose as something he wasn't. Instead, he made funny stories out of his shortcomings.

Common Sense with Missionary Projects

Dr. Bob would take a look at something and assess it. If it didn't make sense, he would have none of it. And he could be scathing at times.

For instance, in 1975 I accompanied Dr. Bob to East Kalimantan (formerly Dutch Borneo). There, a group of nationals were running a Bible school turned over to them ten years earlier when the missionaries had to leave the country. The leaders of this Bible school were eager for Dr. Bob to see the place (he wasn't all that keen to go). The school was away out in the jungle. We went part of the way in an ancient, leaky boat with an outboard motor. (The boat had at least three inches of water in it.) Then there was the climb up the slippery, muddy bank. Between the water and the mud, we were a mess. And what we saw when we did arrive really raised Dr. Bob's ire. The buildings had in no way been maintained over the last twenty-five years. As we were being shown around—I recall the scene vividly—Dr. Bob suddenly said, "Stop! I've seen enough. This place is a pig pen! It's no better than the filthy jungle you all came from." Then with a soft quiet voice, Bob turned to the School director with tears in his eyes and said, "What will it cost to make this Bible school a credit to Jesus Christ and the Bible you are teaching, to make it so that the unsaved will not scoff and say that you might as well have stayed in your jungle village?"

Yes, Dr. Bob was riled at what he saw. But he didn't let that stop him from looking for solutions to the situation. He challenged the men with their responsibility to spruce up the place, and before the transformation was completed, Samaritan's Purse had shelled out about twenty thousand dollars, but the result was a Bible school the Christians could be proud of, a place that honored the Lord Jesus and His gospel.

Dr. Bob hated ruts and was intolerant of people who held to their as-it-was-in-the-beginning-is-now-and-ever-shall-be position. He was creative and original, a risk taker for what he believed God wanted him to do, whether it had been done before or not! This attitude, from which he never veered even in his death bed, sometimes bought him enemies.

It irked Dr. Bob that so few missionaries he met used the Bible culturally. "Jesus was born in *Asia*," he would protest, "and if we would scrape the Western barnacles off the stories Jesus told, they would be readily understood by an Asian audience or individual."

Criticism of his work with orphans, with lepers, and other needy people would cause him to snort, "How can we preach to people who are so hungry, so cold, so sick, so homeless and expect them to listen and respond? Have you never read the book of *James?*" and in a milder tone he'd remind them that taking care of these desperate physical needs is just as much a command of Christ as "Ye must be born again," though he would be quick to add that the latter is of higher priority.

Others who have known him through the years have formed their own opinions—positive and negative—about what made Bob Pierce what he was. Personally, I'm convinced that special God-given abilities are accompanied by certain characteristics—and yes, quirks, too!

Man of Prayer

Many a time I've heard Dr. Bob say, "We so often think that God is not really answering our prayer unless He is relieving us of our pain, or we are escaping from something."

In his fervent desire to spend time in prayer, Dr. Bob wasn't always too considerate of his companions, as my father can testify. Dad has told me of a time that he and Bob Pierce were together and they had to sleep in a tent. They'd had a long day and my father was tired; all he wanted to do was go to sleep. But Bob felt like praying and he did—for four hours, *aloud.*

Others who have spent time with Dr. Bob will likewise long

remember his praying; some tell that he even prayed in his sleep.

One man in particular will never forget Dr. Bob and his praying. That man is Sami Dagher, pastor of Beirut's Karatina Alliance Church. When I introduced Dr. Bob to Sami in 1977, Dr. Bob was immediately impressed with Sami as a man of God.

Since 1976, Lebanon had been embroiled in a vicious, bloody civil war. As a result, the beautiful city of Beirut was divided with the Muslim sector in the West and the Christian sector to the East. Sami lived in the Christian sector; his church was there also, but right on the Green Line—the "no man's land"—that divides the city. Things were in a dire state when, in 1978, just a month before his death, Dr. Bob came at the risk of his own life to visit Sami and encourage him. It was Wednesday and Dr. Bob went with Sami to his church. Right after the church service had ended, the Syrians and Palestinians started shelling the Christian sector of the city. The shelling was so heavy, so intense that when Sami took Bob Pierce back to his hotel in the Western sector, which was under the Syrian/PLO control, Sami was not able to go back to his home. Bob's hotel, like all the others, was filled with people stranded by the shelling. So Sami slept on the floor in Dr. Bob's room.

That was the night, Sami says, that Dr. Pierce taught him how to die. "Franklin," he said, "that was the most unusual, inspiring night I have ever known. For Bob Pierce *prayed all night long!* Hour after hour, as he prayed for people I didn't know—people in his own life—as well as our people under fire that night, the presence of God was so real, so strong in that room, I didn't dare close my eyes. In the midst of my thoughts as to whether my family was safe, I just lay at the feet of this man who was dying, *and who knew how to die;* he taught me how to face death."

That very day, the missionary couple, Harry and Miriam Taylor, who had led Sami to Christ, came under fire. A man knocked at their door; Miriam opened it cautiously to find a man pointing a pistol in her face. She sidestepped the fire, but was almost in hysterics, understandably enough. Later, she said to me, "It was wonderful that Bob Pierce arrived that very day to be with us in our hour of danger and need."

As for Sami, he had despaired of getting Bob safely to his hotel because Dr. Bob was now in a wheel chair which slowed down Sami's ability to dodge the fire. But God had Dr. Bob there that night, and Bob's night of prayer made an indelible mark on this young Lebanese pastor.

I have been with Sami many times since then; always Dr. Bob's prayer is remembered. (Even as we write these words, Sami and his flock at the Karatina church are daily endangered with the current Lebanese/Israeli conflict.) But Sami Dagher knows both how to live with danger, and how to die. His personal prayer is, "Lord, let me die in my strength; don't ever let me get old and cold in my love for You." Sami wants to die like Dr. Bob, trusting and praying.

Personally, I can't recall a time *when Dr. Bob was not praying.* It was his lifeline—he prayed with all the simplicity of a child talking to his father, and he expected results. One prayer Dr. Bob prayed for thirty years was "Lord, let my end be better than my beginning."

Asked by Pat Robertson to pray for the Christians in war-torn Indo-China, his prayer on the 700 Club was:

> Father, we know that You care about all of Your own. We know that You haven't turned Your back, having so loved the world, the whole world, that You gave Your only Son. We know that You haven't forgotten all that have suffered, and we know that You haven't forgotten who He suffered for. We pray for that group, that massive group some place tonight beyond our sight, beyond the coverage of our TV and newspapermen—
>
> We pray for those left behind in Vietnam. We pray for our thousands of Christians, high up in the mountains in the Highlands where so many were saved just the last four, five, six months before Vietnam fell. We pray for our senior, oldest Pastor, who saw his children* on to the plane and out of the country, and then

---

*Even as I was writing this page, my phone rang. The caller, a pastor in Oregon, was none other than the *son* of this brave and devoted Vietnamese pastor.

stayed behind and has never been seen or heard from since the moment the helicopter left until now: he who stayed behind saying, "I must be a good shepherd, not a false shepherd who sees the wolf coming and flees."

Oh God, wherever men stay in the face of almost certain death, wherever they have stayed and they try now to serve You, under all kinds of oppression, all kinds of threat, all kinds of danger. Yes, and martyrdom in cells. Oh, bring up legions of angels to confound the devil, defeat his every scheme, burst through every curtain— iron, steel, bamboo—whatever it may be.

Above all, the curtain of darkness and depression that the devil would bring. Oh God, burst through it all. Thou who art the Light of the World, the Light that shineth in darkness, and the darkness cannot put it out.

Oh God, let Thy Son be present among those untold millions who are under oppression and fear, and hasten the hour when Your promise will be fulfilled that Jesus Christ will be acknowledged throughout the whole earth. Every eye shall see, every tongue shall confess him Lord of Lords, King of Kings, that day when *Jesus shall reign!*

And Lord, we wouldn't pray for these Iron Curtain countries only. We pray for all who are watching right now who have their own "iron curtains" surrounding them: curtains of despair, born out of sin, their own flaws, their own faults, their own failures, and they feel so alone. They don't know that You love sinners. Oh God, burst through now to hear their cry and deliver them—especially those who are oppressed in body and who are oppressed in mind.

Oh Thou Great Deliverer, deliver them also into the certainty of Your love and presence with them. Burst into their hearts and take the throne of their lives! Thank you for hearing our prayer. In Jesus' Name. Amen.

PAT: Thank you. Oh, praise God!

BOB: You know I have one other thing, Pat. I hope that all of our listeners do pray not only for our Christians; we need to remember the unsaved who have never yet had a chance to understand enough about Jesus to make an informed judgment as to whether He is who He says He is. We need to pray that they will have their chance to get enough information to really accept or reject Christ. Many, whom *we* say have rejected Him, maybe God doesn't think so. God knows how much light they have ever had.

The paramount concern of Dr. Bob's prayer was always that souls would be saved—that practical compassion for their needs would earn him the right to share Christ.

Soft Heart / Hard Head

Dr. Bob Pierce had a soft spot in his heart for the national pastors, and he was constantly looking for ways to lift up the national church—ways to help them do the work God had called them to do. One such area was the Pastor's Conferences, for which Dr. Bob Pierce became famous all over the world. However, in the latter part of his ministry (Samaritan's Purse) he did not have the occasion to do this. He did, nevertheless, give criteria and guidelines for doing such a conference in the event that Samaritan's Purse ever did get involved in this area.

Dr. Bob had his rules—his criteria and priorities—for exercising stewardship of God's money. In brief, the following is what he required concerning a Pastor's Conference:

1. Participants must be men of proven worth: if they're not good men, they're of little use. So they should be carefully selected for their spiritual qualities.

2. When we're budgeting for just two from each country, these must be two men. Not a man and his wife. For if one man fails or falls, the other who has had this training, can help lift him up. While we would like the women to know what their husbands are learning, for them to come would mean bringing their children, and not much learning would take place, I'm afraid. And the Bible tells us that *Jesus sent men out two by two.* So that's the best pattern to follow.

3. The students must *not* come for a *vacation.* It's hard study. There will be pleasure, because there will be good Christian fellowship, and as Proverbs says, "It's good and pleasant for the brethren to be together." But the intent of bringing these men long distances is not a time of vacation. It is that they will go back

better equipped through the Word—that they will be more effective in their presentation of it through what they have learned from godly, experienced Bible teachers.

4. The length of the conference/institute/seminar—call it what you will—must be reasonable. One instance comes to mind where the national director was planning six weeks. I said to him, "Well, I want to give you some advice, my brother. I have worked with several conferences where we brought people from many countries together. And if it is more than two or three weeks we find that some get homesick, or some don't want the discipline to be in class every day. So they go home early and we have lost our money. So I refuse to give but *half the money to come* and then they get the money when *they finish* and go home; and I urge you to do that. Because if they come to you after three weeks and say, 'Sorry, we want to go home. We don't like it.' Then you say, 'OK, but you pay your own way. We don't give you one penny. You came. You said you prayed. You said God told you to come, and Dr. Pierce asked God for the money and paid for your fare and you are cheating God. It is God's money. And if you did not truly pray, you came for some other reason; then you must pay your own way home.'

"I ask that this be made very clear to the prospective students, and make sure they understand. Believe me, I learned this lesson the hard way. It has cost us hundreds of dollars to bring a man from another country for training, only to have him come and say after the first week or two, that he wants to go home. He may never have been away from his village in his whole life; everything is new and strange. So we must guard against that kind of thing happening (unless of course, when there are extenuating circumstances). It can be a means of drawing them closer to God, leaning harder on Him, when they are away from home. This too is godly growth.

"So what I'm saying is, we will be financially responsible for qualified men who have prayed and feel confident that God is leading, and that this is the right thing for them to do and who are willing to leave their homes for the specified period. Men who will apply themselves diligently to study and learn how better to preach and teach and witness and live for Christ. For, as a missionary in Bangladesh once remarked, 'Many are *reached* but not all of them are *teached.*'"

It's to help remedy that lack of teaching that Samaritan's Purse began to put into practice these wise, well-thought-out concepts Dr. Bob left for us.

In 1980, I had the opportunity of going through North Borneo and there found a church that had never had a Pastor's Conference since the missionaries had left years earlier. Many of these pastors had not even met one another. With little to nurture or encourage them, some were even leaving the pastorate. We thought if we put together a small conference just for them that this might encourage them.

The church organized the conference and Samaritan's Purse helped financially and provided speakers as well. Rev. Guy Davidson of Tempe, Arizona, and Rev. Roy Gustafson of St. Petersburg, Florida, traveled at their own expense to lead this conference. Jimmy Rim, our Samaritan from Korea who had been working in the Philippines with the refugees, also came to North Borneo to preach. This was the first time these pastors had ever seen a Korean, much less a Christian Korean. (Jimmy is always able to communicate God's Word in a simple but profound manner.) These men of God shared the practicality of God's Word in a direct way that spoke to the hearts of these pastors who had come together for the very first time.

Guy Davidson spoke as a pastor to a pastor. He gave lectures on how to organize one's time, how to put together a sermon outline, etc. Roy Gustafson gave talks on prophecy from the Old Testament as it related to the state of Israel.

The adversaries we faced there were Islam (the major religion), Hinduism, and Buddhism. One young pastor attending the conference shared with us that he had been raised in a Chinese Buddhist home. After he was converted, he refused to eat food which had been offered to idols that were in every room of his parent's home. Of course this caused his family much distress, but God blessed him and later enabled him to graduate from the London Bible Institute. He is now pastoring in the mountains of Borneo.

In the course of our planning for the conference, we learned

that the Evangelical Church in Borneo was represented by a
hundred and eighty churches with less than fifty pastors and *no
transportation*. God impressed upon me that by using a few
motorcycles the pastors could serve more churches. Samaritan's Purse began praying and asking God to supply this
great need. When the time came for me to return to Borneo we
had enough money for five motorcycles.

The day before I left the States, a long-time friend and sup-
porter of the Purse, Fred Dienert*, came to me and said, "I
want to have a part in this project for these pastors; let me buy
three motorcycles." Just minutes before boarding the plane, I
called my office and was informed that someone had sent money for yet another motorcycle. When I reached Malaysia, the
chairman of the church, Arun Selutan, informed me that there
were eleven districts plus their home district, and they already
owned three motorcycles but needed nine more. After chang-
ing the money into Malaysian dollars, we went to the local
Suzuki dealership to see what could be arranged. After careful
negotiations, would you believe we had *exactly enough money
for nine motorcycles*. Our need wasn't for ten bikes or even
eight. He knew the need all along, and He provided.

The motorcycles were presented to the church (Guy Davidson and I couldn't resist riding two of the bikes to the conference). What rejoicing there was among those dear men and
women of God! The smiles on their faces said over and over,
"thank you!" Guy dedicated the bikes to the glory of God. After
the dedication, all the pastors sang, in their own tongue,
praises to God for His provision. I remembered chapter 24 of
Joshua, where Joshua reminded the children of Israel that their
victories were not by their own bow or sword: it was by God's
hand!

Samaritan's Purse will, from time to time, continue to bring

---

*Fred Dienert and Walter F. Bennett were life-long supporters of Dr.
Bob Pierce and the last ten years of Dr. Pierce's life they provided his office
space at their expense so that Dr. Pierce would be free to do what God had
called him to do.

potential teachers of the Word of God to where they can receive the right kind of training. And as good stewards of Jesus
Christ and of the finances entrusted to us by His people, we
find, as did Dr. Bob, that we must blend compassion and
practicality. And I'm sure that Dr. Bob would be pleased to
know that we are seeking to carry on this ministry to nationals—a ministry that was always dear to his heart.

There is no way for us to fully know the complexities of the
man, Bob Pierce. But we can come to a fairly good understanding of him by looking at the life he lived before laying down his
harvesting tools and checking in with the Lord of harvest—by
looking at the things he said and did, at the standards he set for
himself and his organizations, at the things he held dear. For
me, Bob Pierce was the man who called me Buddy, who inspired me, who taught me, who trained me, who left with me a
part of the vision to which he had committed his life—the
Samaritan's Purse.

2. God's Call to a Twelve-Year-Old

AT AGE TWELVE Bob Pierce accepted Christ as his Savior. When he would talk about his boyhood, I recall hearing Dr. Bob say:

> I want to bear witness that there was nothing great in me, a carpenter's son, raised at 339 E. 103rd Street, an area of Los Angeles that later became infamous for the Watt's Riots. There was nobody great in my family—no preachers, lawyers, doctors, or such. God just simply called me to give my heart to Jesus, and I followed Him.
>
> My world was a little Nazarene church about two and a half miles away that, with about every folding chair you could bring in, would seat only about two hundred and fifty. The first time I went to an annual assembly and there were a thousand people, I thought that was more people than there were Christians in the whole world. And I never dreamed of ever leaving Los Angeles, much less the state of California. Like Jeremiah, I complained, "Oh, Lord God, I can't do that. I'm far too young. I'm only a youth."
>
> "Don't say that," He replied, "for you will go wherever I send you and speak whatever I tell you to and don't be afraid of the people for I the Lord will be with you and see you through."
>
> From that time at age twelve, I've sinned, I've quit, I've failed, I've stumbled, I've fallen, I've landed in the mud puddle and come out drenched with mud. But one thing has been true: God set me apart and there's no way that I could run away from God. I have tried. I dropped out for two and a half years one time; went into the shipyards and worked and told the Lord, I won't do another thing!

I won't even go to church. I resign, I give up, I quit, I don't have what it takes, I refuse. God just sat on the sidelines and twiddled His thumbs and said, "Well, when you get ready, what I've planned is going to come about and when you get through kickin' and stompin' and wailin' and feelin' sorry for yourself and blaming everybody else, we'll start where we left off," and that's the way it's been for all these years.

My life verse has been Philippians 2:13, "It is God who works in you both to will and to do His good pleasure."

God said to me, "I'm going to send you; you were chosen; you were sanctified" (and nobody has lived a less sanctified life). I mean I've been hot-tempered, egotistical, hard-driving. I've had to flee to the cross almost every morning . . . get up and beg for grace not to sin anymore and every night I've had to go and ask God to cleanse me with the Blood in order to get to sleep, and that's the way it has been. He has been absolutely faithful. The Scripture says, "Though we are faithless, He remains faithful . . ." (2 Tim. 2:13).

If we don't do our part and He has sovereignly declared He's going to do thus and so, then for His own integrity's sake, He's going to see us through.

As I think back, it astounds me that a young kid of twelve should *positively know* that God had spoken to him as He had to Jeremiah: "before thou camest out of the womb, I sanctified thee, and I ordained thee a prophet unto the nations" (Jer. 1:5).

I was a young Nazarene fellow who had been hurled into the Youth for Christ movement. Fortunately, I got hold of a Scofield Bible which got me off my excuse of eradication doctrine to where I could believe that people other than *Nazarenes* could be saved. And I learned a few verses besides, "*Without holiness no man shall see God.*" (That was the very first verse I ever learned—long before I learned John 3:16.)

The Lord began to broaden my horizons after that. Now I don't mean that I would have become a Billy Graham! He and I did have this thing in common: we were among the twelve founders of Youth for Christ. Bill took Youth for Christ to Europe, and God sent me with Youth for Christ to China, "way back" in those early days.

I never had a desire to be a great preacher; I never wanted to be a famous anything. The passion of my soul since the day God called me to this day—the unbroken chain . . . the *one thing*—has been that I wanted to see men come to the experience of being born again.

There's a cost to that commitment. I found that to be only too true. We sing:

> Where He leads me I will follow—
> I'll go with Him through the judgment—
> I'll go with Him through the Garden—

And I'd like to say, after walking with the Lord forty years and more, that I don't believe we should take—or sing—words lightly.

Having experienced the grace and mercy of God not only in the face of my own failures, but in the greatest heartbreaks and tragedies—the death of my daughter Sharon, the loss of health and of other things—I verily believe that God takes us up on our words, on our promises we say or sing. I believe that God holds us accountable. I'd be afraid now to declare many of the things I've publicly preached for thirty years because, as time has gone by, God has said, "All right. That's what you told everybody else; let's see if that's the price *you're* willing to pay, Bob Pierce."

And I told the Lord that I was willing to forsake father, mother, brother, sister, wife and children, houses and lands. In reality, in one measure or another, it has cost me all these things, and not me only. It cost my dear wife all these things. It cost her a husband to let me just follow the Lord. She never dreamed I was going to be overseas while she stayed in California, and that one trip would turn into five hundred trips, and that one or two months away would turn into twenty-five years of being eight or nine months away. Whenever we make a commitment to God, *especially when we say it in front of witnesses,* I think we must remember that God may put us to the test; and, of course, He puts better people than we are to the test.

My wife, Lorraine, is a spiritual woman. She just couldn't somehow find my lifework and ministry a joy to her as it has always been to me. She loves Christ very much, but my commitment to Him was not the same as her commitment to Him. So, as the years passed, more and more these words of Jesus took on deep meaning for me: "If anyone comes to me and does not hate his father and mother, his wife and children, his brothers and sisters—yes, even his own life—he cannot be my disciple" (Luke 14:26, NIV).

It has cost me all of these. Oh, I still have my life, but it's forfeited to leukemia and my days are numbered. But it's all worthwhile; *everything*. It was the best investment I could ever have made!

It would be good if we could say of Dr. Bob that once having accepted Christ as his Savior and having heard God's call to serve Him, he never looked back. It would be nice—but it wouldn't be true. Bob Pierce never tried to hide the fact that once, in a bitter frame of mind over the conduct of other Christians toward him, he turned his back on all that he had professed, left the Christian ministry and turned to the only trade he had any knowledge of—carpentry. (His father was a carpenter.)

He found the work hard, but that was not the highest price he paid. Here's the way Dr. Bob described that time in his life:

> I let my bitterness, my hatred, my resentment, and all the other things, justified or not, rob me of my position and power and joy with the Lord. God's Kingdom did not suffer, but I did.
>
> People I had led to Christ saw me out there on the job, smoking and cussing and telling off-color jokes and all the rest of the worldly mess. And one day a man came up to me and said, "Five years ago, in the First Nazarene Church in San Diego, I heard you preach and I walked down that aisle and you invited me to come and believe in Jesus Christ. Now here *you* are, living a worse life than I was living when you urged me to give my life to Christ. Now I don't know—what does this do to my faith? I wonder." And he turned and walked away.
>
> Brother, if I'd been a cockroach hit with a sledge hammer, I couldn't have been smashed any flatter!
>
> First, I had to go crawling back to Jesus, then crawl back to my father-in-law . . . crawl back to anything that would bring me peace and let me have power with God again.

God heard His penitent son's cry and He restored him, as He has other men whom He then has used greatly. Who's to say but what this experience made Dr. Bob all the more compassionate toward others who for one reason or another slip away from God for a time!

PART TWO

Dr. Bob's Principles, Priorities, and Strategy

3. The Miracle Ingredient in Faith

WHAT IS FAITH? I posed this loaded three-word question to Dr. Bob on one of our many trips together, realizing I wanted an explanation of the life of faith I had observed in him. He immediately sensed I wanted a careful explanation.

"There's a lot of pat answers to that question, Buddy. That's not what you're looking for and I can't make my answer as short as your question. In my own case, I can look back and pinpoint two or three things. If these had not happened in my life, I don't think God could have used me as He has.

"It was when I was assistant pastor in my father-in-law's church, the Evangelistic Center in Los Angeles. My pay was twenty dollars a week, hardly enough to exist on."

A faraway look came into his eyes as if he were reliving the experiences. Then he continued:

"One Sunday the guest preacher, morning and evening, was Rev. Raymond Richey, who had a consuming concern to win G.I.'s to Jesus. At the close of his powerful message, we took a second offering; this was to help him with his expenses for his tent ministry in areas where there was a big military base. I was moved. I believed in what he was doing to win men to Jesus and when the offering plate came my way, all I had was a twenty-dollar bill—my salary for the week. On impulse, I put it in the plate. As soon as it passed, I was scared at what I had done. How would I tell my wife? And how would I meet the car payment due in a couple days?"

That took great faith on Dr. Bob's part, I commented to myself, *or just plain stupidity.*

"Late that Sunday afternoon," Bob said, going on with his story, "as I was doing some preparation around the church, in came a sailor and his girl. He had his orders to ship out the next day; he had his marriage license, and they wanted to be married right away. Since my father-in-law was not around and I was qualified to do it, after praying with the couple and counseling them a bit on what marriage is in the eyes of God, I performed the ceremony. And, as they left, the young groom slipped an envelope in my hand. Hallelujah! When I opened it, out fluttered a twenty-dollar bill! I got down on my knees and wept, thanking God that He had allowed me to trust Him, feeling ashamed for having had second thoughts and realizing just how weak my faith was."

Bob's faith was honored; he had his twenty-dollar bill back.

"Oh, but there's more," he said, as he went on.

I thought to myself, *keep truckin',* Bob, for I felt God speaking to my own heart.

"Well, in the evening, Rev. Richey was at his strongest and greatest. I had the same impulse again when it was time for the offering. I reasoned, *You gave twenty dollars this morning. God gave it back to you. So you really haven't given Him anything.* So I put the second twenty dollars in the offering."

I was impressed. That took faith. This time I knew better than to think "stupid."

He went on to tell me of his habit of seeking out, after a service, the lonely older people who needed a bit of attention, a little affection and caring. "I didn't have much," he said, "but I could give them that and make them feel like somebody."

That night, one of these women—Dr. Bob said you could only describe her as 'mousey'—as he put his arm around her asked, "Could you please drive me to my apartment and back to church? The Lord has told me to give more to the G.I.'s and my money is at home. I have four hundred dollars set aside for a rainy day, and the Lord has told me to give half to Rev. Richey. I live just a few blocks away."

Along the way, she told him something of her circumstances: her husband was dead and she worked scrubbing floors in the Los Angeles City Hall five nights a week to make a living. "I could have wept," Bob told me. "I wanted to tell her to save her money for when she would need it. But she said the Lord had been good to her in giving her health and strength to work."

Where's all this fit in with your 'faith' story? I wondered to myself, getting impatient to hear the next episode.

Bob went on, "Before that woman got out of my car that evening, she said, 'Bob, I've never had a chance till now to tell you how much it means to me that every Sunday you come around after the service and put your arm around me and ask how things are. I'm not a pretty woman and I have few friends. I come to this church, and I do enjoy Pastor Johnson's sermons and the singing. But what makes me feel so good is that you never forget to come and greet me. I'm so glad I had this chance to talk with you, and now I want you to have this,' and as she walked into the church with me she handed me an envelope. I opened it—and there was a twenty-dollar bill!"

He grinned, then got serious. "I can't give *you* that experience, Franklin. I can't even preach that other folks should ever do it. I don't make any kind of a theology out of it. All I know is that, at a critical time in my life as a young man, I had this experience. It changed my life as to what God would do if He told me to do something and I obeyed.

"Buddy, I know I've gone around Robin Hood's barn to answer your question, but apart from the Scriptures I really don't know what faith is. The Bible tells me it is *the gift of God* (Eph. 2:8). God has to give it to you. It's not something you can acquire by studying comparative religions or anything of the sort. Faith is something God plants in the heart; it *wasn't there*—and you *believe* (as Paul told that Philippian jailor to do)—and suddenly *faith is there*. I'm so glad I know that. For I've stood up to preach and the devil has whispered, 'Pierce, you're a poor preacher; nobody's gonna be saved here this night.' And I would answer, 'You're wrong, Satan. There's

somebody here that God sent. He's not going to be won by any
logic of mine; he's not going to be persuaded by my eloquence
or my exposition of the Scriptures. That person will be saved
because at the right moment by the Holy Spirit using the
Scripture, and the years of faithful praying by the parents, or a
Sunday School teacher's teaching, that spark of faith will be
kindled. Simply believing God, he'll be saved because salvation is *a gift of God* (Eph. 2:8).'

"That was the rock foundation and when later I was out on
my own and things got rough, I could hark back to God's
wonderful provision—for the Word tells me, 'I am the Lord, I
change not' (Mal. 3:6, KJV).

"Hey, Buddy, that reminds me about a step in faith! Let me
tell you a bit about it. Serving as I did in that large Evangelistic
Center, I met a whole parade of the great speakers and singers
of that day. One musical group especially impressed me; they
called themselves the Eureka Jubilee Singers—seven black
singers—and, man, could they sing! Well, one day their pianist
and manager, Mrs. Esther Williams, came to me and said,
'Bob, for five years we have come to this church; we've
watched you and appreciated you. You have the art of leading
singing so that people love you. We feel you would do great as
an evangelist on your own. Why don't you let us travel with
you. We'd be glad to give you three months of our year.'

"I knew it wasn't that they needed bookings," Dr. Bob told
me. "Also, I believed myself that it was time I launched out on
my own. But what about the cost? How would we meet expenses? The Eurekas' weekly bill just for food and accommodations was about seven hundred dollars; then there was the
travel cost."

As Dr. Bob talked, I thought about what I would have done.
I'm afraid my own faith would have fallen short.

"I could write a book just on that experience, Franklin, for
my next step of faith was to *tackle the job*. I took on that singing
group and all our expenses for travel, publicity, etc., when I
had absolutely no capital. I just had guts—and of course the
experiences I've shared with you when God began to teach me

about faith. All I knew for sure was that I was called to be an evangelist and win souls, and I knew that no one else would hire me to do it. There wasn't an organization in the world that would choose me to be the guy to fill their pulpit and pull a big crowd. So we started out together, first in Minneapolis at the Powder Horn Baptist Church that seated just three hundred and fifty. By mid-week I was sick of seeing people standing outside in the snow, then being turned away for lack of room. So I borrowed the money to put a big ad in the newspapers and we booked the Civic Auditorium for Sunday afternoon."

"That's when George Wilson [who is with the Billy Graham Evangelistic Association, Minneapolis] contacted you, isn't it?" I asked.

"Right," he answered. "George heard about our meetings, then saw the ads. He proposed getting the Civic Auditorium for Saturday night and having us. I would speak for Youth for Christ, and they would take a second offering for us. One thing you could count on when the Eureka Jubilee bunch was there, there would be unsaved. And their saved relatives wouldn't have to drag them there; they knew there was always good entertainment with those seven black singers. So we were fishing in a pool that was well stocked; the audience was not comprised of petrified saints. And the word began to go around that we were seein' souls saved at every meeting. Not that I was such a hot-shot preacher, but I sure knew how to give an invitation. I knew, too, that I had made the right choice, to either make a bid to trust God or to drop out. And it took real faith. Many a time my wife could complain, and rightly, so, that when the meetings were over I had paid everybody else, but there was little or nothing left for ourselves. This was when I began to have a taste of daring to do things that take what I call *God Room*."

God Room—I wondered what he meant. I was almost afraid to interrupt his story, but my curiosity got the best of me and I asked, "What do you mean by God Room?"

Dr. Bob looked at me with that disgusted look which implied, "Don't you know *anything?*" With a deep sigh, he said,

"Buddy, in my personal view, *nothing is faith as long as you set your goal only as high as the most intelligent, most informed, and most expert human efforts could reach.*

"For instance, a church sets as its goal one hundred thousand dollars for missions when up till now they've given seventy-five thousand dollars. They form a committee to visit each member, encouraging them to give an additional percentage needed to meet the higher goal. And they do meet it. Okay, that's what human strategy and planning can do; that is what suddenly putting aside lethargy and indifference and raising your sights can do. And there's nothing wrong with doing that. Just don't stop there and call it *faith.*

"But say, that, like a friend of mine, Rev. Guy Davidson, you've built a church from scratch and now it's jammed and you need a much larger building. Your members pledge two hundred thousand dollars for it. And about that time a missionary couple who work in the hell hole of Calcutta come into the community. They attend this church; they don't ask for a thing. But by their lives they begin to influence the whole congregation who begin to shower them with love in return. They offer the couple, Mr. and Mrs. Lamb, a nice place to live and invite them into their homes. Wherever they go the Lambs spread joy and blessing.

"What happened? As the church learned of the appalling needs in Calcutta, the homeless, starving children the missionaries were attempting to care for, they took the entire two hundred thousand dollars pledged for a new church building and gave it to the Lambs! Then these people went to the bank and borrowed the two hundred thousand dollars to replace it. Now *that is faith,* Franklin.

"Even though the devil would come 'round telling them, 'You can't do it; you can't raise another sum like that. You're already in hock and there's no way in the world you're gonna be able to make your payments at the bank.'

"And that's where 'God Room' comes in. Nothing is a miracle until it reaches that area where the very utmost that human effort can do is not enough and God moves in to fill that space between what is possible and *what He wants done that is impossible*—that is 'God Room.' (This is the only phrase of mine that I know is still quoted around the mission fields: 'God Room.') It became a part of my daily life, my daily experience, and my basic philosophy. I emphatically maintain: 'No faith has been exercised until you have promised more than it is possible for you to give.'"

Bob paused, and I promised myself that day that I would never forget his words.

Then I asked, "Do you see any snares in such a commitment?"

Dr. Bob answered, "God Room is a fundamental law with God, though I didn't know that the Sunday I gave Him that forty dollars and He taught me what faith means. Even so, believe me, before you get out on a limb, you're going to think twice about whether this is *really* a God-need, one that is really breaking the heart of God, or not. Otherwise, you're going to be made a fool of, and you're gonna go bankrupt! The guys who don't want to live a life of faith are going to hold you up as an example to prove what a jackass anybody is who opts to live that way—the God-Room way."

My mind was racing to sum up what Bob was trying to teach me, that there is a miracle quality to that kind of faith. I guess that's why most people live and die without ever seeing a miracle or being a part of it. And to think we *can* have a miracle in our lives by daring to trust God for something, undertaking something *He wants done* that's twice what we can do by ourselves, or with the utmost of our resources.

"You need to keep in mind," he cautioned, "that you may not find many who will go along with you on this brand of faith; and we can't impose it on other people. Nevertheless, this ingredient of faith *has to be* the foundation of Samaritan's Purse."

Another way Dr. Bob had of saying this was, "Without the miracle quality, you can get your life and business down to where you don't need God. You can operate exactly like Sears & Roebuck or General Motors or IBM—but the blessings will all be gone. You will be much more conscious of your walk with God when you have that God Room staring you in the face up there unfilled, and you are having to watch God fill it."

That's what made Samaritan's Purse what it is today. If Dr. Bob and those he drew around him had not believed as they did, the whole venture, in spite of Bob's zeal, could have been just a flash in the pan.

Samaritan's Purse, in its first year of operation, raised and dispensed to specific needs twelve thousand dollars. The second year they went out, trusting that God-Room principle, and provided twenty-four thousand dollars to meet critical needs they had promised to meet. The third year it was sixty-four thousand dollars! The Lord was abundantly answering Bob's question, "Will God leave us holding the sack if we believe this is something *He* wants done and we write this check to meet it?"—the answer, *Never.*

Bob was the first to admit that he wasn't always on God's wavelength in these things. "All my life," he said, "I have tried the impossible and often in assinine things. Sometimes God let me fall on my face with a splash that resounded around the world." (Bob wasn't too good on metaphors.) He went on to explain one such incident.

"There's a classic example still going around. I picked up *Christianity Today* a month or so ago and Dr. Carl Henry, who's a good friend of long years' standing, was using it to illustrate a point. It had to do with the Rose Bowl. I'm sure you know that Pasadena's world-famed Rose Bowl seats one hundred thousand. So I had a dream. I wanted us to have an Easter Sunrise service in the Rose Bowl, and Dr. Carl Henry and a few Christian businessmen and others went along with the idea. We advertised all over the place: I put an ad on every streetcar in Los Angeles. (This was some thirty years ago when we had our fine streetcar system.) We hired the policemen and other officials who had to be there. We did every thing possible to assure that this would be a first-class Easter service to glorify the Risen Christ. And I tell you, Franklin, in that 'City of Roses' where it so rarely rains, *it rained* that morning! And you have to be a Southern Californian to know what that does to traffic; cars skid and hydroplane on the streets that are oil-slicked from months of dry weather. People are as loath to go out as if it were a wild snowstorm. So, instead of the one hundred thousand and more we had anticipated, just thirty thousand braved the weather. Oh, we had a great time," he assured me as though living it all over.

"But the thing was, that when it began to cost a lot of money—and everybody (advertisers, the policemen the city insisted on, etc.) had to be paid, as we say now, up front. I had borrowed every cent I could—had even mortgaged my home—to make that dream a reality. And the offering which would, if the crowd had come, have been enough to take care of everything was *six thousand dollars* short!

"What had happened? I don't know. I had felt so sure this was something God wanted me to do. Did I miss His signals? I'm telling you this to show you how important it is, if you're gonna give God all you have, *to be sure it's something He is telling you to do.* A friend was kind enough to lend me the six thousand dollars; and, though it took me nine years, I paid him back every cent."

Dr. Bob could get as discouraged as anybody else, at times. Once, Dr. Bob Cook, realizing that Bob just might quit because of discouragement, encouraged him with this profound yet simple statement, "Ninety-nine percent of succeeding is keeping going." Dr. Bob never forgot that and he passed it on to me.

Another thing he never forgot was what was *God's* doing and what was Bob Pierce's. He'd put it this way:

Whenever you get what you think is a great idea and you say, "Lord, I got this great idea, will you please give me the ten thousand bucks I need so this great idea can be accomplished?", don't expect God to do that. There's no place for God Room there—just ego room.

Bob was hitting the nail on the head. One could spend a lifetime in a seminary and never receive such a lesson. My mind continued to race ahead with a thousand questions; one that I asked was how to motivate people in the churches to latch on to these precepts, to listen and then open their purses or reach for their checkbooks and let God use them.

"You've been there. You've seen the horrors and the desperation, but it's another thing to communicate the need effectively. Is there a secret to that, Dr. Bob?" I asked.

"Yes—all this time we've been discussing what faith is and we needed to; but, you know, Franklin, nobody's ever goin' to see your faith or mine. Faith is something that can't be seen; it can't be touched or handled or analyzed in a test tube. It's what we *do* because of our faith—the kind of things Jesus did out of compassion for the suffering in His day; and, when we do it in His Name, that's *faith in action.*"

"So," I asked, "how do you make that man in the pew *be there* with you, in the leprosy compound or the blind school; how do you let him see and feel the hopelessness of a mother seeing her child slowly starve to death, or a missionary doctor's frustration at being hampered by a lack of surgical equipment, or—oh, a hundred such needs. How do you shake people out of their complacency born of never having gone through any of these things?"

He thought about it for a minute and said, "Well, the only thing I've done about that, these thirty-five years I've tried to serve God in foreign countries, has been to *become a part of the suffering.* I literally felt the *child's blindness,* the *mother's grief.* And there was no way that I could *walk among the lepers and not feel* as lonely, as cut off, as abandoned, as brokenhearted, as debased and humiliated as they were; I wept over the poor little orphan children. It was all too real to me when I stood before an audience. It wasn't just that I had taken notes and shot film; I had *felt* their misery.

"Oh, but I must tell you that this is no quality that *I* developed or worked at feeling," he admitted. "It's a quality I hunt for in other men and women. And it's not something that can be faked. *There's no way to imitate or substitute or counterfeit real feelings. You either feel it or you don't.* And this is, I believe, one of God's gifts to me, Franklin. I *feel.*

"I've never before put into words what the quality is that would never let me walk past (your question has made me think about it). I believe it to be the same quality that made the Good Samaritan stop while the priest and the Levite walked by. They all saw the exact same situation, the man's need. And it was the Samaritan who got off his donkey, saw the bruises and welts and the blood, and could put himself literally inside that body and feel what the wounded man was feeling as he lay there half dead.

"That's the only way I can explain the ability the Lord has given me to cause others to see and feel and rise to meet the need. That's what Samaritan's Purse—and *faith*—is all about.

"Now, I don't mean to imply, Franklin, that I'm some kind of George Mueller [the nineteenth-century evangelist and philanthropist who believed that through faith and prayer God would supply temporal as well as spiritual needs]. I mean, I just stand in awe at the fact that God would ever give me the courage—being nobody other than me, just an ordinary person—to ever try to do something bigger than myself with God as my partner. So many Christians seem to believe that, when the Lord saved them, that's as big as He can do—and they never experience God's power to use them. They miss out on that miracle ingredient."

We concluded our conversation that day in prayer as we did every day. As I went to bed that night pondering Bob's words, I prayed that God would grant to me that simple childlike faith to believe Him and to let the God Room principle become important in my own life.

4. Bob's First Crossroad of Faith

"IT'S ONE THING to define faith for you," Dr. Bob said one day, "but you need to hear about what I call my 'first crossroad of faith': what you do when you're actually faced for the first time with an impossible situation. Believe me, that *is* a crossroad—and you can't just sit there."

I settled back knowing it would be a long story, but not a boring one.

"I had been invited to go to China, my first overseas venture," he began. "To be sure, I was just a substitute. You see, Dr. Torrey Johnson had been the one asked to speak at a big crusade in Shanghai; then he found he couldn't go at that time. I'd prayed, 'Lord, if You want me to go, You'll have to get me there.' I took the Jubilee singers with me and held some meetings up North, expecting that I could raise the money for the trip. But all that was left after expenses was three hundred eighty dollars.

"Another seemingly hopeful avenue [for raising funds] will interest you, for your father [Dr. Billy Graham] was involved with me. It was a great rally at the Hollywood Bowl, and some Youth for Christ men suggested I get up and talk about this China trip and they would take an extra offering to help with the expenses. A feature of that meeting was your dad handing me a Bible engraved:

To Chiang Kai-shek, President of the Republic of China, from Youth for Christ and the young people of America who are praying for you and for the great country of China that it may come to know Christ.

And the next morning there it was on the front page of the Los Angeles newspaper, a large picture of Billy Graham presenting me with that Bible to give to the President. That gave me a great feeling, as you can imagine. But, shortly afterward, the chairman of the rally called to say that, after everything was settled up, there wasn't anything left to help with my China trip!

"What was God doing? What was He trying to tell me? I was to leave the very next morning! And the only thing I was absolutely sure of was that *the Lord wanted me to go.*

"I remember deciding I wasn't gonna go to church and face people who had been in that huge crowd the night before and had heard the announcement that I was going to China right away and had seen them give me the Bible to take to the President of the Republic of China; and then have them figure out that it was all a balloon full of hot air.

"I stayed home all day, sick at heart, asking God why He was making a fool of me. Of course, human nature being what it is, it wasn't *God* I was thinking about, nor the call! It was my punctured self-image: *What would people say?*

"The next morning there was just one thing to do. So I did it. With my wife, our little Sharon, and my father-in-law to see me off, I took my suitcases and headed for the Los Angeles International Airport. That's where I stood and came to the first crossroad about whether I would or would not live by faith.

"People were beginning to check in. I turned to my father-in-law and asked, 'What do you do in a case like this? Here I am and beyond this airport lies the Pacific Ocean. I can't swim. How am I gonna get to Shanghai?'

"He replied, 'At least you can look the Lord in the face and say you came as far as you could. You had this conviction that

He wanted you to go; you had this order from Torrey Johnson [President of Youth for Christ; I was one of their evangelists], and here you are. You can look up and say, "Okay, God. What are *You* going to do about it"?'

"Then, just as I was asking my wife, Lorraine, if she could think of anything I'd left undone, like a flash I remembered that I had neglected to get someone to take a prayer meeting I had promised to speak at while the pastor was absent. Now, I'm sure, Franklin, that God triggered that in my head. I had to do *something* to keep my promise to that pastor, but first it had dawned on me that *I could* go part way on the money I had and trust the Lord for the next lap. So I bought a one-way ticket to Honolulu, the first stop enroute. Then I dashed to make my phone call. I called Wilbur Nelson, Chairman of Youth for Christ, and he agreed to take the meeting for me. Then he said, 'How in the world can you make the trip to China? I know you don't have the money.' So I told him I had enough to take me to Hawaii and $117 left in my pocket. There was silence. Then— and it's as clear to me as if it just happened, Franklin—he said, 'All right, Bob. If you're going like that, trusting the Lord to provide along the way, here's what I'm going to do. I'm going to call every Christian businessman, every YFC committee guy I know, and if I can get together some money I'll wire it to you at the Honolulu airport,' and he hung up.

"Now I need to back up a bit, Franklin," Bob said, and he proceeded to tell me about something that had happened while he was holding meetings a few weeks earlier. At one meeting, a young Filipino man had urged him, if he did go to China, to make a stop in the Philippines. The young man had assured him that an airlines executive, a fine Christian man, would make all the arrangements, and he had given Bob the man's name, adding "Just let him know you're coming."

Having given that background, Bob continued with his story:

"It took eleven hours on that old DC-4 plane from Los Angeles to Hawaii," he said, "and when I got off I didn't stop for anything. I dashed to find the Western Union desk—and hallelujah! There was a telegram for me. God bless Wilbur Nelson and those guys back in Los Angeles. They had scared up *five hundred dollars!* Now I had enough to take me to Manila. So I fished out that man's name and rushed back to the telegraph desk and wired my expected arrival time."

Sometimes Bob's stories would get so exciting I wondered if he didn't make them up as he went along. But I knew better, and I relaxed to listen to the next part.

Bob continued, "I'm still on a flight whose final destination was *Shanghai*, you know. The Lord didn't steer me off my route," he informed me with a grin. "It was a long ride, but we made it and landed in Clark Field. I'd learned that we had aboard a Provincial Governor, which explained the presence of a bunch of cameramen at the foot of the steps. I'll avoid all that, I said to myself, so I hung back and got off last, all rumpled, carrying my old typewriter and whatever else I'd taken aboard. At the bottom of the steps I was greeted by a little man who said, 'Aren't you Bob Pierce?' But before I could answer, I heard '*That's him!* I've seen his picture,' and with that cameras began to click and flash bulbs went off. (I must have had my mouth open in those pictures!) Then along came a man and introduced himself, 'I'm John Sycip. I got your telegram and everything is set up for you . . .'

"'Well, you got the cameramen here,' I chipped in, not knowing what to think about it all.

"He explained, 'That's because you're speaking to the Chamber of Commerce tomorrow in Manila, and I want a little publicity for that.'

"I gasped, 'How in the world—I mean, *I* didn't know for sure I'd get here. How could *you* know?' (And here is where God taught me that I wasn't the only one praying about that 'impossible' trip.) This man said, 'I was just praying. I had a letter from Dr. Torrey Johnson explaining that you might be coming *without knowing how you were going to get here.* I just believed that if you trusted God enough He was going to get you here.'

"He steered me into an old Army jeep, threw my stuff in,

and started driving off. But I knew better; didn't I have to go through Immigration and all that? It seems he had taken care of that, too. He had provided accommodations and was putting a car and driver at my disposal. But first he had to take me to see his fleet of planes. His father, a banker, had set him up in the airline business. John now owned the second largest airline in the islands. I soon learned, however, that business was not John's first priority. He was deeply concerned over the souls of his pilots, not one of whom was a believer yet.

"So I started off by speaking to the Chamber of Commerce. Then for eight days I spoke on a different island each day. John had arranged that a different pilot fly me each time, so I could witness to each one of them.

"It was an unforgettable experience: wonderful crowds . . . who came because I was *American* and our country had given the finest of our men to deliver their islands. I don't know how many were saved in those meetings, but I had a great time. The Americans had left a PA system wherever they had been, so I'd stand up on the highest thing (a truck bed sometimes) and sing my Youth for Christ songs. My biggest hit in those days was 'This Little Light of Mine.' I'd make all the gestures, with my finger as a candle, and they loved it. I was even invited to speak at a Fourth of July celebration. About five thousand came that day. And at the end a priest tugged at my sleeve and asked if I would go with him to talk in private. I'll never forget him. He sat down with me and said:

> I really believe what you preached today, and I want to be saved. I have never experienced what you were talking about, being *born again*. I believe the Bible, and I believe Jesus is Who you say He is, but I never asked Him to come into my heart and really save me; I've never known what it is to know my sins are forgiven.

He was so in earnest. So we knelt down together right there in his little hut, and I led him to Jesus. Now, I shouldn't say *I* led him; he was so ready, and he honestly and fervently sought the Lord on his own.

"Some years later, at a Pastors' Conference in Cebu City, I was the opening speaker and, as I finished and the service was over, a man came out of the crowd and threw his arms around me. 'Do you remember me?' he asked. Then it came to me—that Fourth of July on one of the islands. 'You led me to Christ,' he said with tears in his eyes. He'd had a rough time with his superiors after that; but, fortunately, some students at FEBIAS (Far East Bible Institute of Asian Students) befriended him and helped him get into the Institute. He had graduated from the Institute and had been a pastor for some years and was doing some teaching also. I can still see him and hear him as he said, 'To think that God would let me live to see your face today!' Meantime, I was thanking and praising the Lord for His goodness in so graciously letting me know that something real and lasting had come out of that 'crossroad of faith' trip.

"I wish I could have been as sure of the result of my witness to John Sycip's pilots. He had just depended on me to practically collar those guys and try to bring them to Jesus, which, of course, I didn't do. I just tried to be loving and considerate to them. After all, they did have to sit through my preaching. They had no choice; there was no way to avoid hearing, with the PA system, no place to go, no movies, nothing. They had to sit there and listen to the gospel. I don't know for sure if any one of them ever accepted Christ or not. I just loved them and prayed for them, and they were very warm toward me.

"It was the last evening. I had to leave for China the next day. For some reason I hadn't let John know of my need, that I had no means of getting to Shanghai. He had booked me for that evening in his own Chinese church, a small sanctuary that seated two hundred, and for the first time I spoke through an interpreter. John interpreted for me; and, to my great joy, twenty-seven young people came forward at my invitation. But I have to admit to you, Franklin, that I was dismayed that John had taken no offering."

"That was your last hope?" I suggested, and he nodded assent.

"He just pronounced the benediction and, as the people were leaving, I prayed:

> Lord, You brought me this far, and I want to thank You for what You have done. Thank You for these twenty-seven young people who opened their hearts to You tonight. And, Father, if I never get any further, this is still farther than in my wildest dreams I ever expected to get in my whole lifetime.

But how *was* the Lord going to get me either to China or back home to Los Angeles?"

"That's what I can hardly wait to hear, Dr. Bob," I said eagerly.

"Well, as we left the church John said, 'Let's talk a bit. You know how anxious I am that these pilots of mine come to know the Lord. I know you've preached the gospel each night, and they've heard. But there's one—and he's very dear to me—who because of his tight schedule didn't get to hear you even once. Now I have a request to make. I hate to ask you, but would you be willing to give up your comfortable seat on a regular plane? You see, once a week I send my DC-3 cargo plane to Hong Kong. It goes tomorrow and this man is piloting it. Would you be willing to sit alongside him in the cockpit and talk to him about Jesus on that eight-hour trip to Hong Kong?'

"There was no way he could know I had no 'comfortable seat,' and I didn't tell him. 'Well,' I answered, 'since you put it that way, John.' I'll never know why the Lord had me keep my mouth shut. It's probably the only time that, when I needed money, I didn't make the whole world know it!

"My heart was singing hallelujah that night, and the next morning we took off for Hong Kong. I'd like to report that the pilot listened attentively all the way. But I'd be lying. Every time I tried to bring up anything about the Bible, about God or Jesus, he cleverly evaded the subject. He was a master at that! We arrived and he skillfully navigated that hazardous landing. I was overjoyed to be so far on my way to Shanghai, but I was saddened to know that John's loving plan had not accomplished what he had hoped. We could just keep praying."

So here Bob is in Hong Kong, and I was wondering how I could retell the story without people calling me a liar.

"Now you're in Hong Kong, Dr. Bob. That's still a long way from Shanghai," I questioned.

"That was on my mind, too, Franklin. I'd come a long way, literally, and I had a few crumpled dollar bills and some change jangling in my pocket. But Shanghai was still a far piece to go on that! The pilot had unloaded me and my stuff 'way out on the tarmac—you know about these places—and I'm sighing, Oh, Lord, how'm I gonna get myself and this gear into the terminal? And the sun was baking hot. Right then, the pilot yelled down to me, 'Here. Catch. I forgot to give this to you.' An envelope fluttered out of his hand, and as I picked it up he shouted, 'See that yellow limousine? That car and the driver are yours while you're here. The driver will take you to your hotel.'

"I stuffed the envelope in my pocket and headed for the limousine. 'My hotel' was the luxurious Hong Kong Peninsula, queen of all hotels in that colony; I wouldn't have been able to afford a *cheese sandwich* there. And yet I found myself in a lovely room that John Sycip kept for his frequent business trips. I got down on my knees and just thanked God for another proof of His love and care for me.

"For some reason, the envelope had been blanked out of my mind till then. I got up from my knees, opened it, and *three one-hundred-dollar bills* fell out. Shoutin' hallelujah, I dashed for the elevator and through the lobby to where the China National Air Corporation had an office and, somewhat out of breath, asked, 'When's the next flight to Shanghai and is there a seat left?' That was Tuesday. There was nothing going till Thursday morning, and Thursday evening I was scheduled to speak in Shanghai. I asked the fare. 'Three hundred dollars to Shanghai,' the clerk answered. I laid down my three hundred dollars. I didn't get a cent back nor did I have to pay another cent. I got my ticket.

"My plane arrived at exactly four in the afternoon; and, with the help of an airline fellow who wrote the address in Chinese for me, I headed in a ricksha (no money for a *taxi*) for the China

Inland Mission headquarters. There I learned that Dave Morken, a new missionary whose support I had partially raised by having him travel with me in my California meetings was flat on his back with a jaundice that would keep him down for at least a month. He and I had been slated to work together. I washed my face, and some of the CIM folk took me to the Moore Memorial Church just in time for the first meeting of the crusade.

"It would take a whole book to chronicle all the things God did in churches and on campuses that summer in China. When Dave recovered, we went to seventeen of the largest universities all over China, and I was privileged to speak. Those who kept records tell me that 17,852 men and women not only came forward, but signed cards and were counseled as thoroughly as God could enable us with the means at our disposal. I'm not interested in numbers, Franklin. *One* soul truly won to Christ will have been worth it all."

He paused, and I could tell by the look on his face that he was back there with the Chinese and Dave Morken; then he sort of summed up the whole experience by restating, "I had reached China with almost nothing in my pocket. But I had *a million dollars' worth* of experience to prove that 'Faithful is he that calleth you, who also will do it' (1 Thess. 5:24, KJV). And Joshua 1:9 had new meaning in my life: 'Have I not commanded thee? Be strong and of a good courage; be not afraid, neither be thou dismayed: for the Lord thy God is with thee whithersoever thou goest' (KJV).

"Of all the experiences I had in China, Franklin," Bob said, "learning to trust Christ was the most wonderful of all. He made me trust Him for every stage of the journey. And, each time I had to, my faith was strengthened so that when He brought me face to face with the needs that broke His heart, I wouldn't hesitate to empty my pocket for Him." Then, as if it had just occurred to him, Dr. Bob said something I'll always keep in my heart,

"What if I had *never even gone* to the airport that day!"

Hearing that incredible story of Dr. Bob Pierce's first

crossroad of faith gave me as a young man the willingness to believe that, when you know God's will for your life—when you're sure that *He* has commanded you to do something—in the face of whatever obstacles, whatever "impossibilities", *God's command carries with it the enablement to do it.*

5. Bob's Personal World Vision

BOB PIERCE and I were talking one day when I asked, "Dr. Bob, you've told me about that fantastic trip you made to China—the one you call your first crossroad of faith—now that was in connection with Youth for Christ. So where and when did World Vision come into the picture? Please clear that up for me."

I've learned since that Dr. Bob never tired of telling this story.

"Franklin," he began, "the official records show that World Vision was incorporated in 1950. But in reality my own world vision from God was sparked on that first trip you just mentioned. Let me tell you about that.

"It was when I had a three-day break before my next speaking engagement among university students. With some other guys I'd taken off in an old battered army C-47 war plane on a bumpy dirt field. That C-47 was one of the lousiest planes ever built, but the most reliable for its size and weight. We always called it 'pregnant Annie.' When the Americans went home they left hundreds of those old planes for the Chinese government. That's what I flew on in perfect peace, thinking they were as safe as the DC-3, and the Lord protected me.

"We landed in Kunming in a desolate spot. I got off with my camera and my gear and just stood there, not a living soul in sight except the guys in the plane, and they were ready to take off. There was no activity, nothing but rusting pieces of an aluminum hanger strewing the weed-grown airstrip. Then along bounced an old discarded Army jeep. The stocky driver had a radiant face. She drove alongside and asked, 'You Bob Pierce?'

" 'Yeah,' I said.

" 'I'm Beth Albert. My work is with lepers. Somebody got a wire that you were coming, and I'm the only one who could get away to meet you. We don't know each other, but it's sure nice to have you.'

"I hopped in the jeep, and she drove me to the China Inland Mission Home. We talked a little, and I learned that she, too, was from California. I hadn't been there five minutes when a little Chinese kid with a twisted leg all bent and curved from malnutrition climbed into my lap and I held her, thinking, *poor little girl; where does she fit in here?* Beth Albert answered my unasked question. 'She's mine,' she told me.

" 'Oh, so you're married?' I asked.

" 'No, I just bought her two weeks ago.'

" 'You *bought* her! What d'you mean?'

" 'Well, a mother came here. She had two other children, and they were all starving; so she wanted to sell one of them to save her from dying, and she wanted just two dollars for her. So, to keep her from being sold to some evil man, I borrowed the two dollars and bought her.'

"I knew then that I had met a very special Christian. It broke my heart to see this child who would have been sold to a sex pervert if Beth had not borrowed the money to save her from that fate. She was just as committed to her lepers, I found. The Governor of Kunming Province was a military man, and in order to eliminate leprosy in the city, he had ordered that his soldiers could shoot on sight anyone showing the marks of leprosy, as you would shoot a mad dog. Eight miles or so outside the city the lepers could sit by the highway and beg, their only means of survival. So day after day Beth walked that eight miles to a plot of land the authorities had set aside for lepers. Actually it was a graveyard; the 'scenery' was a stack of coffins. Most of the one hundred twenty there had no shelter.

But resourceful Beth scrounged among the debris left by the G.I.'s: rusting cans, anything she could salvage. She taught those poor miserable people, many of them without fingers, to form mud in the cans and then bake it into bricks in the hot sun. When they had enough, she taught them to make crude little huts to shelter them from the cold at night and from the hot sun in the daytime. After a while they had a village of these little shelters that housed a family, or three or four adults.

"Beth had no help from the outside. The offbeat mission that had sent her was not keeping faith with her. Until we began to support her, she was dependent on whatever some kind missionary in the area felt led to give her. Mostly, though, she supported those lepers through sheer hard work and her own ingenuity. Through it all, she maintained the happiest spirits of anyone I ever met. Among those poor victims of the world's worst disease, she was 'the merry heart that doeth good like a medicine.' She loved the people and they loved her.

"The week Beth arrived, the last of the U.S. officials and the U.S. Consul were leaving the city. The Consul's wife was so moved that Beth was staying on with her lepers when all the other Americans were leaving that she asked if there was anything she could do to help. 'Could you get some chaulmoogra oil and some hypodermic needles?' Beth requested, and the lady did so. That day I visited I saw Beth give one hundred lepers their injection of chaulmoogra (the traditional medication for leprosy until more effective methods of sulphatone were discovered some years later).

"This was the first time these lepers ever had anybody do anything for them. They were the most radiant bunch, and they all became Christians (but not because of any theology). They asked Beth, 'Why are you doing this? Nobody ever did anything like this before.'

"And she said, 'Because I love Jesus and He loves you. He loves you so much He sent me to help you. You are precious to God and God knows you are beautiful. He knows you are valuable, He sent His Son to earth to die for you so that you might be saved and be in heaven with Him and be in a wonderful place and have a wonderful body. He sent me to show you that He loves you, and I love you.'

"Beth prayed with each one and taught them all to sing hymns to her autoharp which she always carried with her. I realized that no matter what her Mission Board did or did not do, God made something out of Beth Albert *because she never backed up* nor fled from danger until the day the Communists came and shot to death the head of the China Inland Mission and had given an edict that every missionary had until sundown to get out of that area. Meantime, she had taught some helpers to give the injections; she had squirreled away vials of the sulphatone in preparation against the day she would have to leave her beloved patients, and she had helped them to beautify their surroundings with flowers, and to grow some of their own food.

"So, Franklin, you see the kind of hundred-percent missionary God used to challenge me to a world vision? But I still hadn't *done* anything about it.

"However, the Lord had other experiences for me!

"The next day Beth drove me in a borrowed jeep to see some others who were doing an impressive work, four German Sisters caring for fifty-two little blind kids whose parents, when they found out their kids were blind, threw them out to die. And all through the war years when Hitler forbade money to be sent for missions, they had carried on. While the G.I.'s were in the country they helped. Somehow they could arrange that some blankets were 'mislaid'; a shipment of food unaccountably missing. But when they left, these Sisters were on their own. They had one sewing machine and with it they made clothes for the coolies, to eke out some income. One of them owned a dentist's drill, and, dressed in her mission garb, she would go out on the street and do dental work to get a little money. They scrubbed and cared for their poor little blind charges.

"I prayed with these kids and did my little Youth for Christ songs and though they didn't understand a word of what I sang, and they could not see what I looked like, still they were fascinated because I was a kind of new sound to them. They could neither see nor understand, but something in my voice must have said to them that somebody else loved them.

"You can imagine that after being there about three days and seeing all this, I'd go to bed at night and say 'God, I am not *doing* anything for anybody. Here are these little people without any help at all. They don't have anybody, and they don't have anything, and You are helping them, and they are doing something, and it makes a difference. These little blind children are being helped, and these lonely unlovely lepers. Oh God, here I am *just making speeches*. I haven't got any money, but they need money. Everybody I've seen here needs money. Beth Albert and these others literally burning up their bodies to take care of these little ones and the suffering ones, and they haven't got anything. *I can't stand it.* I can't give them anything, and they need everything. What am I supposed to do, Lord?'

"And God said to me, 'Just shoot your pictures then tell some folk about it.'

"Well, I shot all the film I had. Fortunately, somebody had given Andrew Gih, my interpreter, one of the early 16-mm movie cameras, and he let me use it.

"But still, Franklin, I couldn't get the picture of these kids and the lepers out of my mind. Beth had nudged me a bit when she asked, 'Bob, can you do something for these children?' Of course I knew I was powerless to do anything about so many— fifty-two of them! But why wouldn't the Lord let me have peace?

"I went on to my appointment in the city of Amoy where I was booked to speak in their famous University. And nearby, on an offshore little island, the Dutch Reformed Church had a school for girls and a hospital. One of the staff, a homey Dutch-American missionary from Grand Rapids, invited me to speak to their girls, 'We have four hundred,' she explained, and told me it would take me just fifteen minutes in a sampan to get there. 'Will you come each morning while you're here?' she asked, and added 'Maybe you can lead some of our girls to Jesus.'

"So for four days, I went out there. The missionary, Tena Hoelkeboer, had heard the simple way in which I taught the university students, and she wanted me to do the same for the children. In the simplest language I knew I told them who Jesus is and how God loves them; that there's not many, but just *one God.* He took the form of an earthly man, Jesus, and gave His life to bear the punishment for any sins they had ever committed. I told them of the wonderful place He has gone to prepare for those who love Him. A place where there will be no tears and where everything is just and pure and good. Then I gave an invitation to any of them who wanted to know this Jesus and to live for Him.

"You know, Franklin, I hadn't brains enough, or insight, to know that there was a cultural difference between Youth for Christ in America and the Chinese way up in the interior of China, so I was preaching the same stuff. I never thought through the differences in their cultural background or how incomprehensible my Western Judeo-Christian ideas and concepts would be to this five-thousand-year-old-culture, with little if any knowledge of even the Ten Commandments. I told these kids, 'Go home and tell your folks you're going to be a Christian.'

"Well, when I came to the mission school the next morning, Tena met me with a little girl in her arms. The child's back was bleeding from the caning her father had given her when she went home and announced that she was a Christian, and she was going to live for the one true God. And Tena didn't say as Beth had, 'Can you do anything for her?' Oh, no! She just threw that little girl right into my arms and lashed out at me. For one thing, she was Dutch Reformed, and while she was very concerned that her girls hear the gospel, she wasn't one for open invitations or altar calls. And worse, I'd gone ahead and done it as if I were home in the States! And this little kid had not only come forward, but she'd gone home and told her father, who was incensed because that by turning to Christ she had dishonored his ancestors. Tena was breathing fire!

"'*You* told this poor little girl to do that,' she stormed. 'Now *you* take care of her. She listened to *you*, she believed what *you* told her, and she obeyed God. Now look at what it's costing her!' She stood there like a general wiping out an ignorant private who had dared to do something without an order.

"'And don't you dare think you can walk off this island without doing something for her. Me? I've got six other little kids already sharing my rice bowl. Now here you've given me one more, Bob Pierce. If you think you can preach like you did and teach your message and then walk off and leave this little girl— well, you're *wrong*. Now, tell me, what *are* you going to do about her?' (not 'can you'; she gave me no option, nor did I want one).

"I stood there with that child in my arms. Tears were running down her cheeks. She was scared to death, so insecure she was shaking in my arms. She was heavy and my arms were getting tired. I was shaken to the core. I had never had such an experience. Nobody had ever challenged the practicality of what I preached! I had never been held accountable for any *consequences* of my message. Now here I was faced with, 'Is what I say *true?* Is there any responsibility involved?' Believe me, you do some thinking at a moment like that.

"I looked down at the frightened child in my arms, and I saw Tena standing there waiting for my answer. I gulped and said, 'I'm not about to run away. But you know that I'm here without any money. All I've got in my pocket is five dollars.'

"'That's fine,' she said, 'you do have your return ticket?'

"'Yeah, I have that, but—'

"'Never mind the buts. Just let me have that five dollars. That'll be fine.'

"'What d'you *mean*, Tena,' I gasped, 'by just fine?'

"She gave me a penetrating look and almost spat out, 'I mean *you are going to take care of this child;* that's what I mean.'

"'Okay, okay—but what will a measly five dollars do?'"

"'Here's what it'll do,' she said in a sergeant-major voice. 'It will buy rice for us all for right now; it will get cloth so she can have another dress and I can wash that one'—she pointed to the bloodstained dress on the poor little kid, 'and it will buy a slate for her for school. That's just the beginning, Bob Pierce. You will send me five dollars every month. I'll let her sleep in the kitchen like my other six do, and I promise you I'll take care of her,' and I knew she was the kind of woman who meant every word she said.

"I looked Tena straight in the eye and said, 'I will.' Then I opened my Bible and took out my pen and wrote her name in my Bible. (I didn't even have sense enough to ask her how to spell that Dutch last name of hers). But there it was, an indelible record that I had made a commitment to God to care for one child.

Dr. Bob paused, and as I was thinking back over the story he had just finished, I was overwhelmed by the dedication and love of these six women—Beth Albert, the four German Sisters, and Tena Hoelkeboer. Then Dr. Bob went on to say, "I didn't know it at the time, Franklin, but in the real, practical sense, World Vision was born that day with Beth Albert when I saw people who, without any support, had proved they loved Jesus and the suffering needy around them—people who loved enough that whether anybody helped them or not, they were going to stay and carry on, serving these people who needed them."

He stopped as though he were reliving that experience, and I almost felt I had been there too, so vivid and real he had made it for me.

"Dr. Bob," I asked, "do you know what happened to those lepers after Beth had to leave? Were they ever heard of again?"

That brought another flood of memories to him. And he began to tell me about the last time he had seen this missionary who had so influenced his own dedication for missions.

"Beth came here to see me not long ago. I have a picture of the two of us right here in this room—two old warriors both going home by the same leukemia route to check in with the

Lord of the harvest. I asked her the question you've just asked me, 'What happened to our lepers?'

"'It may be,' Beth said with her usual good outlook, 'that some of them were able to hide. You know that after you began to support us, some new drugs became available. With World Vision funds I was able to buy a new pill that came out, *Sulfatone*. Remember you had instructed me to give these to every patient no matter what their progress. When I had to leave, they had one year's supply of *Sulfatone* tablets carefully hidden away. That was my one comfort as I had to leave them there at the mercy of the godless communists.'

"'I know how hard that must have been for you,' I said.

"'Yes, but you know, Bob,' she said with that light in her eyes, 'the great hope that I have is that I am going to see them again in heaven. We gave them hope because we preached to them the reality of the resurrection of Jesus Christ, so those maimed hands and those maimed feet and arms would be transformed because of the great, wonderful resurrection power of our Lord Jesus.'

"Franklin, as we said good-bye that day—good-bye until we meet again at Jesus' feet—my heart was glad. I was happy that the Lord had let me be instrumental in supplying some of the tools to help people for whom the Lord Himself showed great compassion while He walked this earth. I should say that Beth Albert didn't quit because she was ousted from China. Before that year was out she had, as she said, 'gone in by the back door, since she couldn't go in the front.' She went to India and burned her life out there for lepers. Like me, she lived with leukemia. And she was in and out of UCLA Medical Center where she radiated her love for the Lord among the doctors and nurses who cared for her. I thank the Lord He let me have a small part in her wonderful ministry.

"And now, Franklin, this brings me to something mighty important."

"What's that, Dr. Bob?" I asked (everything he said was "mighty important" to me).

"Just this," and he was off again.

"As I left Kunming, I told God I'm not going to try and start anything. I'm going to spend the rest of my life finding people like Beth, who even if they hadn't a tool to work with are doing something. I'm going to hunt people who have already proven that they have such a commitment to God. I'm not going to start another organization. I'm going to spend my life backing up people I find—people the world may never think about or care about, but they've proved *they* care about people and God.

"And that basically was what and why World Vision was created: *To meet emergency needs in crisis areas through existing evangelical agencies and individuals.*

"When I could no longer do that through World Vision, that's when I resigned and started Samaritan's Purse so that I could continue to meet emergency needs in crisis areas through existing evangelical mission agencies and national churches.

"It was never in my mind that World Vision would be anything other than supportive," he added, "a purely back-up relationship between those out on the front and a means of supplying some of the wherewithal to get the job done. That and no more was my intent.

"The only measurement, Franklin, I had in assessing what we should be involved in was 'Is this something Jesus would do? Something God would want done?' Ultimately it boiled down to something I wrote in my Bible on Kojedo Island: '*Let my heart be broken with the things that break the heart of God.*'"

He finished that session with another of his wise sayings he had proven through his years of serving the Lord, "*We never do anything well until we know for sure what our aim is.*"

6. My Commission from Dr. Bob

IT WAS JANUARY 21, 1978, a day I can never forget. Knowing that his time was short, Dr. Bob had much he wanted to share with me. Our conversation was taped, but I don't need any cassette to remind me of that day with the man who, next to my own father, has most influenced me and set the course of my life.

Dr. Bob began, "If I had a dying blessing to give you as they did in Old Testament times to one of their family, it would be a prayer that God would grant to you the highest, the noblest aspects of the vision He gave me for the world."

I remember so well that in the middle of telling me something or giving me some instruction he would swing into a prayer:

. . . Lord, You promised that as my days so will my strength be. Well, now here's a day, and it's just one day Franklin and I have together, You know. So I give it to You and I ask You, Lord, give me that strength for this moment. I don't ask that you make my body comfortable. I ask You to make my mind—all these half-dead cells; that You'll charge them, Lord, with something new and fresh and usable. Make my memory function right and help me, Lord, to think Your thoughts and be able to enunciate them clearly. And that'll be enough, Jesus; that'll be good enough, Father.

"And now, Franklin, here's what we need to talk about. I want you to follow me, and earn the right to be heard for Jesus Christ and the cause of missions—"

Again he lapsed into prayer:

> Lord, please talk through me as Franklin and I have this time together. Bless him as You have in the past, and I know that whatever way You want to use him in the future will be worthwhile. I would consider it worthwhile to have lived this extra month if You could in even five minutes do something through me that would bless Franklin's life and make it more fruitful and useful to You. Thank You that he's taken this time from his family and flown all this long way to be here. Don't let it be wasted. Fill the room with Your presence and glory.

It was no light thing to Dr. Bob—and certainly not to me, young as I am—that he was dropping his mantle on me, trusting me with the job of carrying on what he had given his life for.

"Dr. Bob," I said, "what I want you to tell me is what you *feel* about the future of Samaritan's Purse; where you think it should go, what you think it should be involved in—and not involved in. I'd like to have that from you, the founder. I'd like to have it on record from you for myself and for Ted Dienert and for anybody who will later be a part of Samaritan's Purse. I want the *Do's* and the *Do Not's* from you."

He agreed. "I may wander all 'round givin' it to you. But let's start with what *is* a good Samaritan. I want Samaritan's Purse to be exactly what Jesus said it was to be. If we stick to the facts of that story Jesus told, we'll keep on the right track. Who was that Samaritan? Likely a *layman*. The professional religionists, the priests and the Levites, had taken a casual look at the wounded traveler—and gone on their way quite unaffected by his critical need of help. Then along came this Samaritan whom the religionists despised. He, too, looked and compassion welled up in him.

Now, did he look around for someplace he could take an offering to help the poor guy or to pay the innkeeper? No.

"Did he start a building fund for a hospital? No.

"What did he do? He jumped in to meet an existing need immediately, at whatever the cost. First the man had to be moved. So the Samaritan set him up on his donkey, which meant that he, himself, had to walk, leading the donkey and holding up the injured man. This Samaritan *inconvenienced* himself. Not only that, but he committed himself financially. He paid the innkeeper what was the equivalent of a day's wages for a skilled craftsman of his day. Also, there's nothing about establishing a police force to do away with thieves and robbers on the Jericho road. He concentrated on the need at hand, got the man to where he could be helped. And he didn't abandon him at that point, feeling, *Well, I've done all and more than could be expected, for a stranger.* He assured the innkeeper that he'd be back. 'Keep track of your costs; I'll take responsibility for this man,' and he went on his way.

"Franklin, that's the kind we want on the Board of Samaritan's Purse: a man who will put a wounded man on his donkey and he himself walk. Don't tell me about how much money he'll give while he rides in his Cadillac! Tell me what he'll *do without* to meet someone else's great need. That's the story of a *real* Good Samaritan. Something that cost him—and note, Franklin—it's something he can't get back. There was no way this victim of robbers could repay the Samaritan. That didn't enter into his thinking. The need was what grabbed him and moved him to action that cost him something. And notice, it wasn't an ongoing thing. It was a one-time stepping in and meeting a critical need. This differentiates Samaritan's Purse —I mean, *our reason for being*—from what we might call traditional missionary service. I feel our mandate for being is the story Jesus told. He didn't deal in idle tales. What He said back then has meaning for all the world in every generation. I want you to keep this concept uppermost in your mind."

He stopped to collect his thoughts then went on delineating what the board members should be and do.

"Another point I must make, Franklin, is this: I would not want anybody on the board of Samaritan's Purse who is not

willing to go at least once a year to a mission field, at his own
expense. Now, of course we have to be reasonable: some cir-
cumstance might make it impossible some years—illness or an
accident or some such thing. I'm not talking about that. What I
mean is, the man has to have it in his heart—a genuine commitment to God to do it. It may be for just two weeks, okay. But let
him go where the need is the greatest at the moment and let
him come back knowing what we're all about: *why we do what
we do.* I don't want anybody, no matter what his other qualifications, who will not do that! I want him to have this kind of
vision because he's personally aware of the hurts that make
people bleed, aware of the plight of the 'little' people; he needs
to feel the awful frustration of missionaries who have given
their lives to serve Christ, yet their hands are tied because of
lack of tools to do the job. All this, Franklin, has to be the
burden of our board members. Nothing less.

   "I don't know what problems we'll confront in the future, or
what needs will arise. All I want is men who've earned the right
to deal with these problems because they've sacrificed, they've
traveled, they've listened, they've shared suffering. Above all
else, whatever they saw and comprehended of need, when
they got home *they did something about it.*

   "Oh, I need to add this. I'm willing for a guy not to be willing
to risk his life if he's got a wife and kids at home, or a church for
which he's responsible. But I'm *not* willing for him not to go
and let the bugs have their chance to bite him! To go to see
exactly how some missionaries live. It's okay with me for him *to
set the limits* at which he's willing to risk his life. I thought I
should make that clear. It's true, not everybody has more than
a certain amount of courage, and we shouldn't look down on
them for that. I just happen to be a guy that was born without
fear."

   Bob was being realistic. How else can we get a *feel*, a realization of the need *ourselves*, so that we can do something about
it, and be practical about letting other people know unless we
go to a mission field and experience the need firsthand?

   "Now here's another principle," he continued. "Samaritan's

Purse will keep a flag flying high that will always characterize us. That flag is *Jesus Christ*. No matter what Samaritan's Purse does, whether for lepers in India, the Mission Aviation Fellowship, the sidewalk dwellers in Calcutta, or victims of flood or earthquake or famine in Guatemala or Africa or Bangladesh— *anything* we do or have a part in doing—we do *in the name of the Lord Jesus Christ*. This must always be. God forbid that we ever do anything in the name of 'do goodism.' May our stand be that of Paul, '. . . this one thing I do . . . I press toward the mark for the prize of the high calling of God in Jesus Christ.'" (Phil. 3:13,14).

Even now I marvel at the strength the Lord gave Dr. Bob as he so vigorously voiced his principles and unchanging expectations of Samaritan's Purse. God certainly answered his prayer for clarity of mind as well as for "strength for this day." "Keep that flag flying, Franklin. That's the core of it all." And again he closed his eyes and prayed,

> Oh, God, fit Franklin to not only be a sharp tool with a bite for Jesus, but Lord, fit him to undergird fainting warriors for Christ.

The more he prayed for me, the smaller I felt, the more totally dependent on God.

"One more thing," he continued, "we never trust in the arm of flesh. That can be deceitful and dishonoring to the name of Jesus Christ." Then he defined for me specifically what he meant. And his definition showed that he was a realist as well as a man of great vision.

"Now by 'the arm of flesh' I don't mean that we don't use expert services. For instance, if we're going to drill a well out there in the Seychelle Islands or a desert in North Africa or some such place, we're gonna hire some geologists who know where the water is. And we're going to call in the engineers who can bring up the water. But what I'm saying—and this is vitally important, Franklin; don't ever forget it—is that when we hire these people we want them to wear the armband of whatever company they're with, not the armband of

Samaritan's Purse (and possibly by their behavior dishonor Jesus Christ). I want them to be paid and let it be said that Samaritan's Purse, out of love for the Lord and to help meet a dire need, got this thing done, and they employed the Amalgamated Association of Sand Engineers, or whoever, to do a certain part of it. Don't pretend that it was *Samaritan's Purse* engineers who did it. D'you get the point I'm making? I want Samaritan's Purse to stay true to Jesus Christ 'til the day He comes."

He stopped as though trying to recall another point. Then with a vigorous shake of his forefinger at me, he passed on this admonition:

"One way to guard against slipping from our *God-Room* moorings, Franklin, is by never, *never* accepting aid from the government; no grants from any government. 'Who pays the piper, calls the tune,' you know; I will not be beholden to any officials by having them subsidize the work the Lord gave Samaritan's Purse to do. Now I'm all for fostering good relationships with these people in high places—don't get me wrong! In fact this has opened many strategic doors for me in foreign countries. But get into any kind of financial deal with them, put ourselves in any such bind!—No, *sir;* no way can we *ever* let ourselves be snared into that trap! I've seen what this kind of thing can do to the faith principle—and I want none of it.

"I haven't come to the matter of giving as it concerns our board members. We need to talk about that. I want, on the Samaritan's Purse Board, men who are willing to go the second and even the third mile in giving. There are plenty of men who would be willing to have their name on our letterhead, but who would never give of themselves or their money. Money was an integral part of the story Jesus told about that Samaritan.

"Let me be quick to say, Franklin, that we're for *churches;* we're for tithing—but we're for more than that. The Pharisees and the Levites were careful to tithe. They tithed to the letter of the law, even down to the little spices they used. Moreover, *Jesus said they should!* I don't mean I'd make it a rule. I don't want to force anybody to give. What I mean is that anybody, board member or employee, should be with us enough to *give*. They have to believe in us enough for that. The year I founded Samaritan's Purse our total budget was twelve thousand dollars, and two thousand dollars of that was from an insurance policy I cashed in, in order to get it started. There has been no year since, that the Lord hasn't enabled me to give twenty to thirty percent of whatever income I had. It was a joy to give to the limit. And that's the kind of men and women we want with us, Franklin. If they don't believe in us enough to want to give—give cheerfully and much—then they're not the people we want with us. That's how it has to be if we're gonna stick to our purpose for being. We want people who'll give as that Samaritan gave—without expecting to be repaid. This is contrary to what some TV preachers are teaching, exploiting people to get them to give by telling them 'You give your dollar to God, and He'll give you back two dollars.' That's the wrong reason for giving altogether, according to the Good Samaritan story. I believe it's the wrong reason by every biblical injunction. We ought to give to God because we love Him, and it ought to cost us something. Like that time when David made up his mind to erect an altar to God at a certain place. He went to the owner of the threshing floor—you know that story in 2 Samuel—and wanted to buy the place, and when the owner heard what David wanted it for he offered it for nothing. But David said, 'Will I offer . . . unto the Lord my God of that which doth cost me nothing?'—and he paid the price.

"That's how we've operated these years, and that's how it has to be in the future. You'll need board members who will be true blue at the end as well as in the beginning. So I pray you will have these kind of men whose commitment to Jesus Christ has been already proven: men who care about the lost, about human needs—genuine, really genuine followers of Christ who listen to His voice.

"Franklin, you can be prepared to have some well-meaning folk ask the question, 'If the most important thing in the world is getting people *saved*, why are you so involved in spending time and money for food and clothing and sick people and orphans?' This always brings to my mind Lil Dickson, that heroic missionary in Taiwan. Lil had two answers for that question. Someone would challenge her, 'If you're here as a missionary, why are you taking care of orphans and giving clothes to these mountain people? You should be busy *giving out tracts.*' Lil would reply, 'I must first meet their immediate needs, then I can meet their greatest need.' What was she *saying?* 'When a little child is homeless, cold, and hungry, we must provide care; and how can we expect a man, who's standing there shaking in the cold mountain air, to pay attention while you tell him about Jesus—especially when you're introducing a concept he has no background for understanding?' That was her first answer. Her second, and maybe it should be our first, was that *Jesus commands us* to feed the hungry, care for the widow and orphan, heal the sick, cleanse the leper, prepare a portion for whom nothing has been prepared. There's no honest way around this, Franklin. I don't want someone tellin' me what the Greek says, and expecting me to hand out tracts to people who can't read yet, or who are too cold and hungry to care about a tract. It takes both—showing the compassion Jesus showed and giving them the simple gospel. I've found that before we can hammer home even the heart of the gospel, John 3:16, the *fact* of God's love has to be driven home by a demonstration of love. Here's something I've proven: almost all heathen cultures absolutely cannot fathom or comprehend a total nonrelative doing something for them— an act that's wholly unselfish and done to meet their need or alleviate their suffering. They're suspicious that there's some evil design behind the seemingly kind act. So we need to prepare the hearts—earn the right to be heard—before we try to preach Christ to people who have never once heard of Him."

Once again, Dr. Bob had "driven home" his point. He was so practical and every word made sense. Each conversation with him was like a breath of fresh air, and I was eager to take it all in.

7. Criteria for Medical Good Samaritans

DR. BOB ALWAYS HAD fixed standards for the things he put his heart into. I well remember the day he laid out for me in his forthright manner what he would expect and insist on regarding medical doctors who would function alongside Samaritan's Purse.

I was about to graduate from Appalachian State University in Boone, North Carolina, when two surgeon brothers, Doctors Lowell and Richard Furman came to me and said, "We understand that you know quite a bit about the mission field—you've traveled with Bob Pierce and you have worked overseas. Could you help us set up an organization that would send Christian doctors to mission hospitals for short periods? Generally speaking, four to six weeks."

I informed them that what I knew about missions they could put in a thimble. The fact that I had traveled with Bob Pierce and worked overseas with missionaries did not qualify me as a mission expert. Furthermore, I told them that I thought they were trying to reinvent the wheel, and that there were probably many organizations that sent Christian doctors to mission hospitals for short periods of time. They were not aware of these and asked if I would help them to research to determine if, in fact, there was a need. I refused at first, telling them that I was planning to go to California and work for Dr. Bob Pierce and Samaritan's Purse and that I did not want to get tied down with some other organization. However, the younger brother,

Richard, kept insisting and the wheels began to turn in my head. I was a business major, and I was approaching the summer. I could either go to summer school or I could do an internship. I went to the two brothers one day and said, "Listen, I'll be willing to do research for you men to see whether organizations like what you are thinking about are in existence and if not, is one needed? I will do all this if you will work it out with the university so that I can get school credit. I don't want to take a dime from you fellas 'cause I don't want to owe you anything." They agreed and worked out the necessary arrangements with the university.

I wrote twenty-one different mission organizations, and I asked them two questions: If we were to set up an organization that would send Christian doctors to your hospitals, would you use us? Secondly, do you know of anybody else that is doing this? While I was waiting for their answers, I thought I should go and talk to Dr. Bob Pierce. I had to go to California anyway, and I thought this would be a great opportunity to pick his brain. I told Dr. Pierce that the brothers wanted to set up an organization that would send out Christian doctors to mission hospitals, but I felt that they did not know exactly what they were getting themselves into. I felt they needed a little direction to keep them out of trouble. So I asked Dr. Pierce, "Could you help?" I explained that one of the brothers, Lowell, was already in India working in a hospital. This was his first trip, and I thought when he returned, he would be better informed of the opportunities and problems than before he went. The other brother, Dick, was a thoracic surgeon; he was getting ready to go and had already talked to a pacemaker manufacturer in this country who had donated fifty pacemakers for him to take to India. Dr. Bob seemed interested but made no comment—at first. I went on to tell him that there were fourteen other men who had similar interests and that they might be willing to go to the field once a year. My concern was that these men did not really know how to discern where the critical needs were. I didn't want to see them go somewhere and waste their time. Furthermore, it was my opinion that if doctors were going to go, they would need to be willing to be witnesses for Christ. Even though they may not be directly involved in preaching, they should be willing to share their faith in Christ with whomever they come in contact—even if it is just to say "I am a Christian, and it is because Jesus died for me that I am here providing medical services to you." I asked Dr. Bob, "Do you think it is possible and do you think that this is something Samaritan's Purse should be involved in?"

Dr. Bob sighed and had a kind of "not-possible" look. He began, "Maybe it would work—if they would be willing initially to take an extensive trip to a number of hospitals, not committing themselves to any one of them, no matter how great the need until they had surveyed all the places on their itinerary. I'd say possibly going to Papua New Guinea, Kalimantan, and Bangladesh. They can cover all these in six weeks. I know, for I've done it."

You may be questioning, why would such a compassionate man as Bob Pierce insist that these doctors keep on going to other places when surely there must have been needs they could have met at any one of these locations? And I'll grant you, that is a fair question. But this is where Dr. Bob's rare insight comes in. He knew from having been in all of these places that almost any doctor would be tempted to remain the whole six weeks at the first stop. He would then never get the opportunity to move on to where the need might be much more desperate and far less likely to be met. Bob Pierce had learned not to sacrifice a future ministry on the altar of a much less needy one that's immediate. He had learned the hard way. "Ninety-nine percent of the guys who ever undertake such a survey," he argued, "just get to the first hospital—and often, it is the next one down the line that has the greater need." Dr. Bob went on to explain that if these men wait till they have covered the territory they plan on, then when they return home, they can make some educated decisions as to going back to which places. They would know what the needs are, and they would have consulted with the doctor in charge to learn what it would be best to bring. "It just makes sense all around to make that first exploratory trip," he said.

I chipped in, "Dick is getting ready to go to India, maybe he would be willing to meet you somewhere in the world and let you give him a little extra tour to some of the critical places, where the gospel is on 'the cutting edge.'" Dr. Bob said, 'Yeah, we could meet in Bangladesh, just a two-hour flight to Dacca from Calcutta and we could look around some hospitals there. They have over ninety million people in that little country. Then maybe on the way back we could go to Bangkok and see that hospital up North we helped rebuild thirty years ago when I was with World Vision."

I said, "Dr. Bob, that is exactly what I am talking about. These men don't quite know where to go—they've got willing hearts; they are wanting to do something, but they don't know where and how to proceed. They don't know any of what you have just shared with me, Dr. Bob: they don't know people who are aware of where the need is and who can help line things up for them. Take for example a hospital, whose missionary doctor is so tired that he cannot keep up with the surgery and a backlog develops: he is desperate for help. Maybe one of our doctors could go out and relieve him so the missionary doctor could get caught up on his sleep and let our doctors take the night calls, all the weekend calls, so he could be with his family, and rest. Or, maybe the need is for a kidney specialist or heart surgeon. God could use us to have the right doctor there within a couple of months or less."

At this point Dr. Pierce started to get excited. He said, "Buddy, it's *really* Samaritan's Purse kind of stuff. It's a meeting-emergency-needs-kind-of-thing. That's what we are all about. Obeying Jesus' command—and He does command us to heal the sick. Your doctor group fits right in there."

But Dr. Bob wasn't through with his stipulations. He wanted me to make sure these men were really intent on meeting a need, not just on having some kind of adventure, as he had known some to be.

"And if these doctors are serious enough that they would like to create a medical arm of Samaritan's Purse and, in effect, get people out of ditches," he said, "at least two of them, the potential leaders, ought to make this one survey. In micro-cosm, by visiting in those places we've named, they would see some of the greatest medical needs in the world. That would shake them up enough to confirm their call. In Irian Jaya they'd find three hospitals with just one doctor, a U.S. doctor—and you wouldn't even call any of the three a clinic. But they would get an idea of what the problems are.

"So, my answer to your question, Franklin is, *'Oh God, bring this to pass, but bring it about so it won't be a flash in the pan.'"*

I asked Dr. Bob, "If some of these doctors went on their own to different hospitals, could they pick up some of this informa-tion on their own?" He thought this over before answering. Then, shaking his head he said, "I don't believe they could do it on their own, even if we especially selected the best hospitals for this purpose. And here's why, Buddy. You *can't get* the kind of knowledge you need by just going the rounds of pa-tients and talking with the doctors. There's more to it than that. You have to get the background of the patients . . .

"And here is where the man's real concern for the people themselves—not just for their illness or disease—comes to the fore.

"A doctor can diagnose the main disease that brought the patient to this hospital, but they have no way of knowing the conditions that have contributed to it. They can tell if the patient is infested with worms, or if he's had TB for years, or if he is dying of a heart condition. But until they've seen the villages, the hovels and all that makes up these people's daily lives, the doctor never knows the five thousand other things that contribute to the success or failure of their efforts. And if they just stay within the confines of the hospital—well, what I'm saying, Franklin, is that I don't want any doctor going just to perform surgery. He must care about the *people* them-selves, not just their *physical ailments*. It's a whole different world out in the villages. The doctor needs to know something of the filth, the germs—yes, even something of the rituals and other things that contribute to the complications that can follow surgery. A doctor, to be able to do the best he can for these 'little' people, needs to have some of this know-how. And there's just one way to get it.

"Oh, I'm not puttin' down any of these good men you've been telling me about. But I've known some doctors who were just looking for some bizzare hospital experience to talk about when they got home. Or—maybe they were combining adventure with a tax write-off!" (Bob Pierce could be cynical, but it was experience that had bred this attitude. He was only thinking of the "little" people and what's best for them.)

"We want those who are genuinely interested in the people" he said. "There will be those who will say that I'm just not appreciative that they're willing to go and operate and even witness to the patients. And I'll have to say 'that's right, if that's all you're interested in doing.'"

Dr. Bob was really wound up on this. I could see he was arguing from a position of reality. These were indeed things that had to be taken into consideration. He had been around for thirty years in those areas. He knew the pitfalls—what worked and what didn't work.

I pursued my questions: "If we can find two doctors who are willing to do all these things—who understand why they're important—do you think it's possible to set up a trip within a month?"

"Yep," he nodded. "I know the very guys—Mission Aviation Fellowship (MAF) pilots—who would fly them to the very kind of places we're talkin' about."

My next question brought an equally positive response. I said, "Do you foresee any kind of problem with the personnel? Would the doctor there accept an outside doctor who comes for a couple of days or so to survey? Can we be sure they'd like that?"

"With these MAF guys flying them in—with our long-standing relationship with MAF! Why, those hospitals, many of them, are absolutely dependent on MAF. They're their *lifeline.* No problem there, I assure you."

Next, he brought up the point of the visiting doctors themselves and *their* attitudes. "Suppose a doctor from the States shows up and acts superior and looks down his nose at the facilities—he's just come for a little spiritual adventure, and he doesn't appreciate the colleague who doesn't have any multi-million dollar research units and all the rest. That kind of thing creates friction, the same as it would any place else."

(I didn't want to interrupt his train of thought, but it came to me, Isn't this a two-way street: *wouldn't the staff surgeons out there have to be very understanding, not looking down their noses at the "raw" visiting surgeon because everything was new and unfamiliar to him?*)

"So, early in the game," Dr. Bob continued, "they need to be humble enough to say why they've come: and that is to be a servant of Christ and to learn from these missionary doctors. They don't go in saying, 'Now this is what I'm going to do'; instead they admit, 'I want to do something useful for God. And I've come to see what it takes out here to do it, and if I have the guts to pay the price.' That can be hard to admit, for especially in this country, we invest the doctor with superhuman qualities. It's hard for them not to have a giant ego, unless they stay humble before the Lord. But if they're going to do a worthwhile piece of work themselves and, by their cooperative spirit, build up the doctor on the field, they can be of untold value and blessing on almost every mission field in the world. Yes, I'd welcome such men, and women, too. God bless the women doctors and nurses. God's work would grind to a halt without them."

This particular visit with Dr. Bob was a great day, for out of it several things emerged. One, Bob and I put into motion a plan to take Dick Furman on a trip to New Guinea after he completed his work in India. Bob said he would take him to some of the most remote areas of the world where he could see first-hand the needs of an island of millions with absolutely no medical facilities. Also out of that day emerged World Medical

Mission. This would be an organization which would function with the same Board as Samaritan's Purse, having the same goals and purposes—meeting emergency needs in crisis areas through existing evangelical agencies, (in this case, hospitals and clinics).

Has it worked? Did we find doctors, men and women with the commitment to match Dr. Bob's criteria?

Oh yes! He didn't live long enough to see World Medical Mission at work (though who's to say that he hasn't been aware, from his vantage point in heaven, of what these dedicated doctors have done and are doing?).

They have gone—men and women "standing in the gap" to where there was a dire need—to remote parts of Africa, to a jungle hospital in Bangladesh; they've jumped in to stem a cholera epidemic; they've relieved a hard-pressed missionary surgeon so that he could spend some time with the family while the children were home from boarding school; wherever the appeals have come from, if it was at all possible, some member of the World Medical Mission group has volunteered. They go at their own expense, often taking wife and family with them. The wives have worked right alongside when their skills permitted, and the children, besides having their mission horizons broadened, have made their own contribution. Families are especially appreciated in most of these cultures.

One of the doctors, as he left home, couldn't know that God would use him as a Good Samaritan before he ever reached his destination. Delay caused by bad weather was responsible for him missing his connection out of New York. But that proved to be a God-ordained delay, for he had to take a plane other than the one on which he was scheduled. Just one and a half hours after take-off, over the PA system came the call, "Is there a doctor on board?" Responding, our doctor found a man suffering a severe heart attack. He administered medication, but with his years of experience as a thoracic surgeon, he realized this man would not survive the flight to London and notified the captain who immediately arranged for an emergency landing in Halifax, Nova Scotia, and for an ambulance to meet them. Meanwhile our doctor shared with the sick man the love of Christ. This man managed to reach into his pocket and gave our doctor a card. When our doctor returned, we were able to follow up. And I am happy to say that the man recovered, and has attended my father's crusades in the city where he lives. Not only is this so, but in appreciation for his life being saved (for he would have died on that plane), he has made sizable contributions to Samaritan's Purse.

God needs *medical* Good Samaritans, and I'm happy that we have this fitting combination of Samaritan's Purse and World Medical Mission, with the same purpose, the same goals—to spread abroad the love of Christ and win men and women to Him.

I think back to the day when Dr. Bob felt it was vital he should tell me all these things that were on his heart. Even in his weakened condition this was all-important to him. And I thank God for this man's insights, and for sharing with me what it would take me maybe forty years to learn for myself.

And as we work on the logistics, do the planning, and pray these godly surgeons out to the needy field, then rejoice with them as they come back and report to us, in my mind, I see Dr. Bob smiling and nodding to me and saying, *"That's Samaritan's Purse stuff*, Buddy; that fits right in. They're being obedient to Christ's command to heal the sick in His name."

Bob Pierce burned his body out physically during the Vietnam War. This picture reveals the strain on Dr. Bob at that time.

Bob Pierce and his family, left to right: Sharon, Lorraine (wife), Bob, and Marilee—1957.

Bob Pierce being honored on "This Is Your Life"—April 9, 1961.

Lord, thank you for this food—and please protect me from it!

Dr. Bob Pierce preaching at Young-Nak Presbyterian Church, Seoul, Korea. Dr. Han (to Bob's left) interpreting.

Bob Pierce inspecting the slums of Jakarta.

Dr. Pierce directing one of his films in Korea.

Wang Ming Dau, former pastor
of one of the largest churches in
China prior to Communist
takeover who spent over 25 years
in prison for his faith. Dr. Bob,
at his death, thought Wang Ming
Dau was dead. The Western
world was surprised and
overjoyed to learn in 1980 that
Wang Ming Dau was alive and
had just been released from
prison. This photograph was
taken by Roy Gustafson, team
evangelist for the Billy Graham
Evangelistic Association—1981.

Beth Albert

"Borneo Bob" reading his Bible
by lamplight in the wee hours
of the morning in the jungles of
Borneo. Photo taken by
Dr. Bob Pierce—1977.

Dr. Bob with his Korean orphans.

Philippine Pastor's Conference—October 30–November 3, 1967.

Below: *Bob Pierce holds child of leper parents at Taipei Leper Colony, Taiwan.*
Right: *Dr. Pierce poses with one of the recipients of the many wheelchairs donated by World Vision to Vietnamese amputees.*

Bob Pierce preaching to American troops at Korean front. Dr. Billy Graham to the right with head bowed.

Left: Dr. Bob receives Medal for Public Welfare Service from Korean President Syngman Rhee—May 7, 1959. Below: Seoul, Korea Crusade—1957.

Left: Bob Pierce with Prime Minister Nehru of India.
Below: President Diem of Vietnam greets Dr. Pierce.

Below: President Miguel Ydigoras Fuentes of Guatemala greets Dr. Pierce at the Presidential Palace during Pastor's Conference—January 22–27, 1962.

Dr. Pierce, General Chiang Kai-shek, Billy Graham, and Madame Chiang Kai-shek.

Bob Pierce interviews Dale Evans during one of his many radio broadcasts.

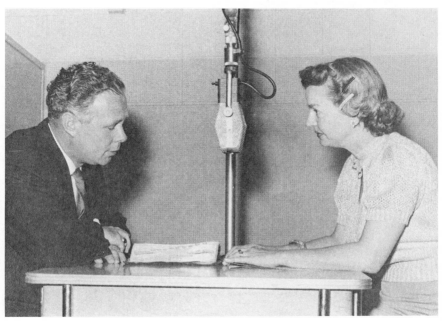

Above: First time white man had ever been to this New Guinea village. Bob Pierce explains "faith of a mustard seed."

Above: Bob Pierce taking one of his last flights with MAF—1977.
Left: Dick Furman, Bob Pierce, and Franklin Graham—Soba, New Guinea—1978.

Bob Pierce on his way to preach—Suluwesi, Indonesia.

PART THREE

Dr. Bob Remembers

8. Heroes of the Cross Who Fueled Dr. Bob's Fire

FROM HIS EARLIEST experiences overseas, Dr. Bob was inspired and motivated by what he observed in the lives of certain missionaries who crossed his path.

One of these missionaries was introduced in chapter 5—nurse Beth Albert. She was the one whom Dr. Bob called "my beloved partner and fellow warrior, the one who was probably the most powerful trigger of the vision God gave me for world missions."

A Hundred Percent for God

It seems more than a coincidence, then, that Beth should also have been the subject of Jeanette Lockerbie's first published article.

Curious about this woman who had so influenced Bob Pierce's ministry, I asked Jeanette what made *this* missionary so outstanding, and this is what she had to say:

"Beth was 'a hundred percenter,' Franklin. That was the title of my article: *A Hundred Percent for God.* Let me tell you about it quickly (it would take a book to tell all I know about Beth). We had met when she made her first deputation trip to Canada. My husband had arranged the meetings with his pastor friends and I escorted Beth, a Californian, on a two-week tour. She always prefaced her missionary presentation with her conversion testimony. It was a graphic account, and I began to tease her, 'Beth, it must be true, for you say the same thing every time.'

"Beth Albert had been a student nurse at Huntington Memorial Hospital (five minutes from where I live now in Pasadena, California). There was an active Nurses Christian Fellowship chapter and Beth kept refusing invitations to attend their meetings. At last, 'to get them out of her hair,' she consented to go—but 'just once'! And as soon as the meeting ended she made a beeline for the door. However, the sponsor beat her to it and said, 'Beth, you impress me as a person who is a hundred percent for anything you do; wouldn't you like to be a hundred percent for God?'

"It might as well have been the voice of God, for Beth never got away from those words. On night duty, her shoes seemed to be tapping out a hundred percent for God—a hundred percent for God—a hundred percent for God, along the hushed halls. To add to her feelings of unease, on three successive nights following that NCF meeting, a patient died! Beth, a compassionate girl, tried to console the grieving relatives. But her usual words of comfort had a hollow ring to her now. She could not forget the words of that NCF speaker: 'Jesus said, "Ye shall . . . die in your sins: whither I go, ye cannot come."'" [John 8:21, KJV] And that *hundred percent for God* haunted her.

"By the third morning, she turned over the patient charts to the day nurse who relieved her; then, instead of going to breakfast, she rushed to her room. There, on her knees, she cried, 'God, if you are real, *be real to me now*—and I promise I *will* be a hundred percent for You.'

"God met her need—and she kept her vow.

"Exactly six months later, attending a compulsory lecture, she heard a representative of a Leprosy Mission appealing for nurses. The Lord spoke to her, 'That's what I want *you* to do,' and she readily responded, 'Lord, if that's what You want me to do, I'll do it, and I'll go wherever You send me.'

"Another thing I appreciated about Beth Albert, Franklin,

was that she didn't wait till she crossed an ocean before becoming a missionary. She began with her own family, her sister and brother-in-law, Mina and Glenn Serres, being her first targets. She witnessed faithfully; then, as Mina says, 'Beth could go off to China and leave our salvation in the Lord's hands and know we would be saved.'

"Beth was also an inveterate Navigator memorizer; and, like Bob Pierce, she spent a lot of time in prayer. I roomed with her for two weeks, so I know. She has been a tremendous inspiration to me from the first day I met her in the train station in Montreal to the very last days of her life. Even now I continue to be inspired by the life she lived. In those two weeks I roomed with her, she kept me laughing probably more than I have at any other time in my life.

"Beth completed her R.N., then took two years of Bible training at The Bible Institute of Los Angeles (now Biola University). After that she spent some time in Carville, Louisiana, studying leprosy medicine and techniques. The time was immediately after the Second World War, and in the Philippines leprosy was rampant. With her up-to-date training and methods, Beth worked in the Islands for some months, then proceeded to China. And that's where Dr. Bob met her.

"It was no wonder he was impressed with her, Franklin. Beth was by all standards the most dauntless, ingenious, level-headed Christian I've ever met; and at the same time, she was the most joyful and the merriest. I dedicated my book, *The Image of Joy*, to her.

"We last met (she spent a couple of days with me) the same week that she and Dr. Bob visited and taped their reminiscences. She, too, was suffering physically. The doctor who examined her at UCLA Medical Center said, of all the patients he'd ever seen, she had about as much wrong with her as any of them. She had served Christ among leprosy victims for twenty-six years after being forced out of China by the Communists. She never spared herself. Even in her final days she was working with International Students in Los Angeles, and died witnessing to her doctors.

"On their last visit together, Bob Pierce said to her, 'I'm not a missionary, but I own a little stock in half a dozen projects of one kind or another overseas; I have a little piece of stock in you, Beth. How I praise the Lord for this. I am going to clip coupons in heaven forever on these little investments I made.'

"That meeting took place on February 24, 1978. Bob went home to be with the Lord on September 6 of that year; and Beth, who had looked forward to returning to India even though her body was so ravaged, was called into the presence of the Lord just fifteen days later—September 21.

"I couldn't help thinking, Franklin," Jeanette continued, "as I sat in the memorial service for Beth in her home church, San Gabriel Union, *Beth welcomed Bob Pierce to Kunming, China; now he can welcome her to heaven.*"

I Bought *You*

For fifteen years Dr. Bob used his radio program as a platform for missionaries to tell their story. One such missionary was Gladys Aylward. Gladys started out an unknown; "small" in every sense of the word—except for her *faith*. She was catapulted into world view through the movie, *The Inn of the Sixth Happiness* which portrayed her phenomenal work with Chinese orphans, and the book, *The Small Woman*, the story of Gladys Aylward.

Because her life had made such an impact on Dr. Bob, he wanted his radio audience to meet her, so he invited her to join him on a program during a furlough time in the States. The following is that interview:

DR. BOB: How does God pick the people He uses, Gladys. For instance, how did He choose you?

GLADYS: I don't think God calls just anyone, Dr. Pierce. I believe He has His *plan* and the *place* and the *person* He is fitting to do a specific work in a particular place. He had in mind a little place in the heart of China, a job to be done there, and He led me to it.

DR. BOB: You're British, right?

GLADYS: Yes, and a more unlikely missionary to China there never was! When God called me, He knew I had little education, no experience, no social standing (I was a domestic—a *chambermaid*); no church would back me; no missionary society would send me. Yet I knew then, and I'm still as positive that God called me.

DR. BOB: Many of us have read about how you worked so hard and saved every penny, then took that hazardous, uncomfortable long trip, traveling in the lowest class across Russia and into China. And there you ended up caring for *eighty-three children*. The story of how you led them on foot, at great personal danger, to a place of safety is well known, Gladys. What I'd like you to tell me and my listeners is: How did you happen to take on the care of these little children?

GLADYS: Well, I had been in China about two and a half years and I was feeling lonely. The nearest foreigners were a three-days' journey away and I rarely saw them. So first I asked God for a husband, and He didn't send one. Then I asked Him for a fellow-worker—and He didn't send any. So I began to think, *Gladys Aylward, God has just forgotten all about you here in this place all by yourself.*

DR. BOB: Now you know our God would *never* do that; but I know the feeling. So, to go on . . .

GLADYS: Oh, I'll never forget it. I was walking along the main street of our little town—it just had one street—when I saw a mountain woman and beside her as she sat cross-legged a small, miserable-looking, filthy child. I couldn't tell whether boy or girl. It was blazing hot and I stepped up to her and bent down and said, "Don't you realize that if you sit here and let the broiling sun beat down on your child's head much longer the child will *die?*" She looked up and with a shrug said, "It's no business of yours if it lives or dies. And if it dies I'll soon have another." I was aghast. Then I figured I just misunderstood (it would have been easy, with so many mountain dialects). But something inside said, No, she really did mean it. But how could any mother be so totally inhuman! Then I concluded that this was not the child's own mother. I just stood there looking puzzled and suddenly the woman looked up and said, "Do you want it?"—not *he*—not *she*—*it*.

"You can have it for two dollars."

"No," I said, "I *don't* want it—and I don't have two dollars," and I walked off thinking, *You surely can't buy* anybody for two dollars! Anyway that child was going to die, and it would take a dollar and a half to bury it—and I just didn't have that kind of money, I argued with myself. No—no—*no*—I didn't want it. As I started on my way, the woman began to shout after me, "A dollar and a half—you can have it for a dollar and a half." No! I insisted to myself.

DR. BOB: So you somehow were able to let that poor child go. How, then, did you get so involved as to have eighty-three children on your hands?

GLADYS: No, Dr. Pierce. You see, when a few hours later I came back that way, there they were still. The woman saw me coming and looked up and said, "O lady-with-a-half-pity, here I am. Do you still want it?" I snapped, "I didn't want it before, and *I don't want it now!* Anyway, I told you I don't have the money—"

She interrupted, "A dollar—a *dollar,* you can have it for one dollar." Then I was sure the child was going to die. The price had been cut. But my mind was made up. Being very Chinesy, I was going to say, very politely as a Chinese would, "I don't want it," and walk on home. But, Dr. Pierce, the words were just half out of my mouth when something happened. I can't explain it—neither can I forget it, *ever.* It was as if someone brushed lightly against me. I didn't see anybody; I felt something. Was it the wind? But, no. We don't have wind in the middle of a town or city. Then it was as if a voice close by was saying, "You don't want it—but *I* do."

My mind asked, "Who are you?" and the answer came, "Oh, I'm the One who bought you." Then I knew. I couldn't see; I couldn't hear; I just knew that it was the Lord Jesus. But I still was saying, "I can't buy that child; I don't have the money."

And He said, "Yes, you do. Right in your pocket." And I realized that I did have some Chinese coppers in my pocket, but that money was to buy something for me to eat. I don't want to spend it to buy something I *don't want*, I argued with myself; after all, I had climbed up a mountain, perspiring all the way and had gotten all the people together and preached to them till I was hoarse. Now I needed these coppers to buy some dinner.

And the voice said, "I know all about it, Gladys. One day I climbed a mountain; I perspired all the way, and when I got to the top of that mountain, I let men nail me to a cross. And I died. It was for *you*. I never argued about money or tomorrow's dinner; I just paid with my life's blood. All I'm asking you is that you take your few Chinese coppers that mean so much to you and buy a little body whose soul I can save." I tell you, I felt like a worm. Hurriedly I turned to the woman and astonished her by saying, "I'm not bargaining. I have ninety cents. You take it or leave it."

DR. BOB: What a *story!* How did you handle the child? Tell me something more.

GLADYS: We went home, and we didn't have a pleasant time. The child curled up in a little ball and went to sleep off by herself. I cried myself to sleep. In the morning I set a bowl of food out for her, and she ate just like a little animal. But, bit by bit, we drew nearer, and we learned to love each other. Now I don't think we loved each other because we believed in each other. *She* loved me because I had bought her; I loved *her* because I had bought her. I didn't pay that ninety cents because I loved children. I bought that child because *the Lord Jesus bought me*, and I truly believed He was asking me to buy her. The love was born through my buying her.

DR. BOB: The love of God shed abroad in our hearts is what makes us act a little bit like Jesus. Now, friend, I know that soon you had other children; and I remember you told me that it was definitely settled in your mind that *forty* was the absolute limit. Yet, *The Inn of the Sixth Happiness* shows you with your eighty-three.* I'm interested in what happened to change your intentions. Because you see, Gladys, we at World Vision never intended to have thirteen thousand children—or anything like that number in our orphanages either. We felt if we could take responsibility for three or at the most four hundred that would be all we could handle. Will you tell all those folks out there who are listening to you as eagerly as I am, why and how you came by all those other children. You didn't buy *them*, too? How'd you end up with twice as many as you vowed you'd keep?

GLADYS: Our plans are not God's plans. In my thinking I had money enough, love enough, room enough for only forty—no more. But I've learned that when God sends the child He sends the love, the money, and the space to provide for the child. The amazing part to me is that the little ones who came later weren't brought in by me; they were brought one by one by some of the forty who were already there. They who had never before known a home and love and now both were theirs, they were the ones who brought others in various ways. Now that they knew love, they wanted to pour it on to someone else who had been like they were.

That's how I happened to have many of the extra forty I never intended to have. They would bring a scrawny, half-starved child and hold him up and say, "Look! He is so small, he'll take up just a little room," or, "You're surely not going to turn this poor baby away." I would find they were collaborating in this: one would bring the child and the others had already promised to share with it. This would be their way of introducing him and saying so wistfully, "We *can* keep just one more, can't we?" And I ended up with the eighty-three.

DR. BOB: Isn't it wonderful that people who have never known compassion until Christ reveals love and compassion to them, want, for the first time in their lives, to show compassion to others. Thank you, thank you so very much for coming. We

---

*At a later date, Dr. Bob learned that the figure had climbed to one hundred three.

will never forget you, Miss Gladys Aylward, and what the Lord
Jesus is doing through you. And I'm nominating you, not the
"small woman," but God's *Great Woman!*

*Dr. Bob used his radio ministry to lift up and promote oth-
ers, for the glory of Jesus Christ. It was never his intent to
pump up himself. Dr. Bob invested in the work that God had
given to Gladys Aylward by giving her a platform from which
to speak.*

Death to the Teacher!

Korea was a country which Dr. Bob loved and to which he
gave much of his life. The Korean War produced thousands of
widows and orphans. When Dr. Bob saw the need of these
women and children, he formed World Vision to help them.
Bob could tell thousands of stories concerning this great land
and its brave people. One story I remember his telling was
"Death to the Teacher!"

Mr. Kim was a teacher in a government high school and died
on the school ground. His crime? He had organized Bible
classes and encouraged some four hundred young people who
had just given their hearts to Jesus Christ.

Dr. Bob Pierce had just spoken in that high school a short
time earlier and the principal, himself a believer, had said,
"Before you finish, tell them *how to become a Christian.*" Dr.
Bob did, and about four hundred young people stayed after the
others had left. He told them all he could in the hour he had,
but then had to walk away.

Immediately Dr. Bob sought for a man who could do follow-
up, and he learned that right in the meeting was a teacher who
loved these young people—one whom the students respected
and who was a Christian. That teacher was Mr. Kim—a man
who from that time forward gave many hours every week to
special Bible studies for these four hundred students. He was
doing great work; the young people were growing in the
Lord—when suddenly came that awful day in June, 1950!

As Dr. Bob recalled that day, he said, "Without warning, the Communists struck—pouring into South Korea. Within three or four days, the schools were taken over; and, in a week's time, they were weeding out the 'unreliable' teachers. There was no way of knowing that they had been making lists not only of all Christian pastors, but also of all the educators. Some students got wind of the fact that their beloved teacher was on that hit list; but, before he could do anything, the Communists seized him for an example that would intimidate others. They lined up the students with his Bible class right in the forefront. With the Communist leaders and leftist teachers and students, they held a 'Teachers' Court.'

"There Mr. Kim stood as accusations were hurled against him: he had committed the 'social crime' of organizing Bible classes and teaching the young people who flocked to them. Before sentencing him, they stuck him up on a platform with a microphone in front of him and demanded, 'Speak! Inform these young people that all you have been telling them is *lies*— that the reason you've told them these things is that you are a spy for the Americans.' With that, a Communist soldier was ordered up, a bayonet jammed into the teacher's back till it slashed his clothing, as with a rude shove an official screamed at him, 'Come on! Speak up, or *die*. Tell the truth or you will die!'

"Slowly Mr. Kim straightened up and faced his young students.

"'All right,' he began, 'I'll tell you the truth. And I want you to *never forget* that it *is* the truth. I did tell you about Jesus Christ, that He is the Son of God, that He came to die to save you from your sin, that He forgives and transforms us and gives peace that nothing can destroy—not even losing everything in the world . . . not even *death*. I told you these things. But now our people are dying, our homes are being destroyed, the countryside trampled and ravished. Now comes the hour when people are asking if there *is* a God who cares, if Jesus Christ *is* the Son of God, if He *does* save.'

"He paused, then in a loud voice—as though he would speak in capitals and underline every word—he declared, 'Yes! Jesus *is the Son of God*. He does forgive sins. And even at the moment of death a man can know that God is his Father and heaven is his home; that nothing else matters; and that *there are things worth dying for*. There is *peace*. Jesus gives peace and confidence and hope! I tell you this: everything I have taught you is *true*. Never, *never* forget that.'

"For this courageous, triumphant stand for Christ, they sentenced Mr. Kim to death. They dragged him away to the back of the school where they dug a hole. But, before they could kill him, he cried out, 'I'm a *Christian* and I want to pray before I die.' Then like Stephen, the first Christian martyr, Mr. Kim prayed for those who stood as his accusers, asked God to forgive them, even as they poised to fire the shot that would end his life. As he finished his prayer, an officer barked a command and, in the sight of the loyal Christian young people who loved him, a bullet shot through their teacher's body.

"This man gave his life for Christ, something I've never been called on to do. And I can never forget that this heroic teacher was sentenced to death for his faithfulness in following up the young people *who had professed Christ in my meetings!* He nurtured the sheep that had been my little lambs, took them to be a shepherd to them, and gave his life for them."*

God's Real McCoy

Dr. Bob had heroes of all ages. Here he tells about a preacher whose church board was about to consign him to a retirement home in Florida when God called him to sell all he owned and go to India.

———————

*This story is based on an interview Bob Pierce had with Dr. Han Chung Chik whose special ministry was with widows and orphans. Through Dr. Han, Bob was able to find and then to support Mr. Kim's widow and his children.

"It was Madame Chiang Kai-shek who first told me about seventy-two-year-old Dr. Charles McCoy," Dr. Bob said.

"How did she know about him? Well, their pastor, himself an old man, had met and been so impressed with the tall, white-haired, godly American that he had invited him to come along to the Generalissimo's (President Chiang Kai-shek's) private chapel. 'He didn't dare invite him to preach without my husband's permission,' the Madame told me and added, 'But Dr. McCoy *did* preach.' She explained that, after the regular sermon, which was brief because her husband didn't like long sermons, the pastor called on Dr. McCoy for the benediction.

"Madame continued, 'He stood and raised his hand, then prayed as I'd never heard anyone pray for our country before. He pleaded for wisdom for the leaders, reminding God that many of them are His people; he prayed for my husband and me, for our army, for our poor people who are living in fear; for God to confound the plans of the enemy. On and on he prayed and I *wept,* as I heard him. At the same time, I was afraid for what my husband might be thinking. You see, he does not understand English. Would he feel imposed upon? Then, as I glanced at him, I saw tears running down his cheeks. Even without knowing the words, there was no way anyone could doubt that this man was talking to God—and *God was listening.* Far from being angry, my husband turned and whispered to me, "bring him home to lunch with us."'"

Dr. Bob went on to say, "now it was the following Sunday. I had preached and been invited 'home to lunch' and the Madame said, 'He sat last Sunday right where you are sitting today.'

"You better believe I wanted to meet this man! And it happened that he, too, was staying with Jim and Lil Dickson. (They had said they had another guest, 'a very interesting old man,' but I had not met him the night before when I arrived.)

"He was an impressive figure of a man, 6-feet-4 inches at least. I heard the most phenomenal story from him. He had been pastoring a church in Oyster Bay, New York (once a very high society area on Long Island—President Teddy Roosevelt had a home there). Now here he was at age seventy-two, with seven university degrees, among them a Ph.D. from Columbia and a Ph.D. from Dartmouth. His denomination, Baptist, had mandated that he retire. He had never married, just cared for his mother as long as she lived. But now what?

"Dr. McCoy said, 'I just lay on my bed thinking that my life's over, and I haven't really done anything yet. I've been pastor of this church for so many years and nobody really wants me much—and what have I done for *Christ?* I've spent an awful lot of time working for degrees, but what does that count for? I haven't won very many people to the Lord.'

"I could agree with Dr. McCoy about these priorities, but I was impatient to hear what changed everything for him. 'So, how come you're here in Taiwan and preaching to the Generalissimo?' I asked. *It was a far piece from Oyster Bay,* I was thinking.

"Dr. McCoy continued his story: 'It was like this,' he began. 'A week after I was asked to retire, I met a Christian brother from India and, on impulse, asked him to come and preach for me. He did and after the service, he said in a matter-of-fact voice that he had preached for me; now why didn't I come and preach for them in India? *Just like that,* Dr. Pierce.

"'But I told him I was *old.* I was seventy-two and my church had just notified me that I had to retire, and they were about to shunt me off to an old people's home in Florida which I'd hate.

"'He interrupted me and said that I shouldn't go to Florida. He explained that in India they begin to respect a man when his hair turns white. And he repeated his invitation for me to come to India. I thanked him and dismissed it at that.

"'But again, lying awake, I couldn't rid myself of the feeling that life was over. Once in, I'd never get out of that retirement home. And it was then the Lord spoke and told me to go to India. Oh, I argued that I didn't have any money—I'd never traveled even across America—I couldn't go to India. But the Lord said, You *can.* Just sell your car and all those things around your house that you and your mother accumulated. There was no way I could mistake it. God wanted me to go to India.'

"'How did that church that figured you were too old for them take to the idea of your heading off to India?' I asked.

"'Oh,' he said, 'they all wanted to take steps to protect me from my folly. They shook their heads and made dire predictions. "What if you *die* in India?" the young chairman of the board asked.'

"I will never forget Dr. McCoy's answer.

"'It's just as close to heaven from there as it is from here.'

"He told me he did sell his car and practically everything else and booked a one-way passage to India. With all his earthly goods in just one trunk, this seventy-two-year-old preacher, who had never been on a ship—or even on a plane—boarded that ship and sailed for Bombay. When he disembarked after that long journey halfway around the world, he found that his trunk was lost. All he had besides the clothes on his back were his passport, his wallet with a little money in it, and an address of missionaries in that city (he'd clipped the address from a missionary magazine before he left home). Clutching the little piece of paper in his hand, he sought for someone who could speak English and could give him directions. A man pointed out a streetcar and explained where Dr. McCoy should get off. But when he stepped off that crowded car, he found that both his passport and his wallet were gone! His one comfort as he stood there stunned was that he'd held the paper with the address in his hand all the time. Heading for the right house, he told his story to the missionaries, who commiserated with him and welcomed him to stay with them. Now he didn't know a soul in India. The man who had invited him was still in the States—was possibly going to remain there.

Dr. Bob continued, "The missionaries who were dear people didn't know what to do with this great hulk of a man. Then a day or so later, he announced, that he was going to see the Mayor. They cautioned that the Mayor was a pretty important man and that they had been there for years and had never

gotten to see him. That was all right with Dr. McCoy, but since
he had come this far, he'd decided he might as well see some
big people. He told them that *he had prayed about it*, and then
he set off on foot for the City Hall, saying to himself, *If he'll see
me, fine. If he won't, he won't.*

"The clerk at the desk sized him up, then asked for his card.
(You have to have a business card in these countries or they
think you're a nobody and that makes it hard to get anywhere
with them.) She glanced at it, the degrees and credentials and
so on, then excused herself. In minutes she was back and
wanted to know what was the business he had with the Mayor.
Dr. McCoy told her about his being a student and then a
teacher in the major American universities and about being a
minister of Jesus Christ, but that he had never till then been
out of the United States, and now he wanted to tell the Mayor
about Jesus Christ. He laid it all out. Again she disappeared for
a few minutes, then returned full of apologies. 'Mr. Mayor is so
very sorry that he cannot see you just now; but if you will please
come back at three o'clock, he will receive you.'

"And receive him he did. That Mayor, seeing the Ph.D.'s
and so on, and hearing from the clerk about how impressive
and tall the man was, and about his white hair, figured he
might be a representative of the President of the United States
or some other dignitary. He wasn't gonna take any chances, so
he'd called together all the big officials in Bombay for a tea in
Dr. McCoy's honor.

"When they had been introduced, the Mayor said, 'I understand that you are an eminent scholar and that you are interested in our country; that this is your first time abroad and
that you really came to talk to us about Jesus Christ. We are
honored, sir. Please go ahead.' That dauntless old man spoke
for thirty minutes, gave his testimony, told what Jesus meant
to him; and, when he finished, they all politely applauded.
This was a group of cultured, university-trained men treating
an elderly, educated visitor with respect and courtesy. Or—
they may have been just trying to get rid of him. No matter.
As he was leaving, a tall distinguished man in a uniform

approached him and asked, 'Could you find a time to come and address the students in my school, sir?'

" 'I'm here because God sent me to serve your country,' Dr. McCoy replied. So a time was set for the following Thursday. A car came for him and he arrived to find that 'the school' was India's *West Point*—The National Defense Academy at Poona (near Bombay) where Indian officers are trained. He addressed that student body of young cadets and he was so full of love— that he was invited back four weeks in a row.

"Word began to get around the missionary community (who up till now were just being kind to 'an eccentric old man') that the Mayor had held a reception for this unknown Dr. McCoy and the commanding officer of the Academy had invited him not once, but four times to speak to his men about Jesus Christ. So he began to be invited everyplace!

"For sixteen years—until he reached the age of eighty-eight—this godly man circled the world preaching the gospel of Jesus Christ. In Calcutta, there's a Chinese church that resulted from his faithful preaching and teaching; in Hong Kong, as a result of protracted meetings he held when he baptized over thirty new believers, there's a healthy witnessing church.

"Dr. McCoy never had any more money than to get him from place to place. He would let us, his friends, know where he was heading, and we would send along some funds to keep him going. One time he was going to Cairo for four or five weeks; and, as usual, some letters were awaiting him. But there was a Suez crisis at the time and the government confiscated all the foreign mail. Now, *there just aren't a lot of fundamentalist Christians in Cairo for a needy brother to turn to!* It wasn't all that pleasant with the Egyptians, but the Lord was with him and saw him through many rough experiences. He finally got out by way of Lebanon.

"I remember a later incident concerning this dear brother. I was with Walter Corlett at the Carey Memorial Church in Calcutta. It was just shortly after I arrived that Walter and I walked out on the street in front of the church and a pedicab was approaching with a huge man spillin' over each side as the 'driver' ran along pulling it.

"'That's Dr. McCoy,' I exclaimed, as the pedicab sailed right by. We shouted at him. If God had not sent Dr. Corlett and me out at that very time, he would have missed the Church; would probably never have found it in that teeming city. He was to preach in Calcutta, then go on to Hong Kong— and God had put in my pocket the money for his fare to Hong Kong.

"It was a few years later, when he was eighty-eight years old that Dr. McCoy was once again in Calcutta. He'd been preaching on a weekday afternoon someplace, and Brother Corlett drove him to the Grand Hotel where he was staying. As Dr. McCoy got out of the car, he said to Walter, 'You know I'm speaking tonight at the YMCA. That's at 7 o'clock; it's 4:30 now, so I'll just have time for a cup of tea and a bit of rest. I don't want to be late for that meeting, Walter,' he emphasized; and Walter Corlett said, 'I'll be here in plenty of time, brother,' and drove off.

"Dr. McCoy walked into the hotel, took the elevator to his floor and—nobody knows exactly what happened after that. But the Lord took him home.

"No one saw it happen. Nobody saw the homegoing of that dear eighty-eight-year-old brother who had just finished preaching and wanted a little rest and refreshment before he got ready to preach again.

"He had come to the end of his great adventure. He was as close to heaven as if he had never left New York. He had been faithful; he had put God to the test. He had tackled something bigger than any man could do, even though he would often say, 'I started when I had nothing to lose.'"

The Prisoner of Kojedo

Dr. Bob's status as a United Nations War Correspondent (and that's another story!) gave him access to places missionaries could not go. The Island of Kojedo was one such place and there, he states, "I found one of the greatest stories of heroism I ever heard—the story of supreme love for Jesus Christ in the midst of extreme suffering.

"I had gone to visit my beloved friend Harold Voelkel, a Presbyterian missionary of heroic heart and soul. When other missionaries were being evicted, he reverted to his World War II army chaplaincy role by re-enlisting; and, because he was fluent in the Korean language, he had been assigned to this prisoner-of-war island.

"When I arrived I found he was keeping up the Korean Christian custom of early morning prayer meetings, with hundreds of prisoners standing outside before sun-up in that bitter winter cold. Their favorite hymn was 'Jesus Loves Me,' the little children's hymn. I'll never forget it—morning after morning by five-thirty all those men standing in rank inside that barbed wire.

"I asked Harold how this Christian worship got started in this prison, and he told me about a wonderful Korean brother who was here as a result of a misunderstanding. This was his second imprisonment. He was a humble little man who had found peace through Jesus Christ and had left the rice paddies and grain fields to serve Him. He'd gone to Bible School at the great Presbyterian Center in Pyongyang, but he didn't have a college-level education. He was pastoring a small church when the Communists came in. At first they were friendly to religion because the North Korean church was so strong: almost three thousand churches in North Korea. But they soon began to tighten the screws, to try to turn pastors and churches into propaganda instruments as a means of controlling the grassroots people. When they took over Pastor Im's village, they recognized they could never force this man into their mold; so, without even letting him see his wife and children, they just picked him up in the village, arrested him, and sent him to prison. For eighteen months he didn't know what had happened to his wife and family.

"Then the day came when General Douglas MacArthur with U.S. and U.N. troops and tanks crossed the 38th parallel into

North Korea and took the capital city of Pyongyang. They
released the prisoners, among them Pastor Im who had just
one thought: to go home and find out about his family. Ragged
and unwashed, he started out on foot as fast as he could, north-
ward to his home. Along the way, he was mistaken for a Communist by the American forces in the area. They saw him as
running away because they had captured the Communist capital. He didn't know a word of English; the Americans didn't
know a word of Korean; and the pastor was given no opportunity to explain through an interpreter. They arrested him
and threw him into prison on the windswept island of Kojedo,
locked in with thousands of other North Korean prisoners.
Because the guards suspected that any gathering was to plot
something, it was dangerous for a group to get together. Machine guns and barbed wire were everywhere.

"Treated like a Communist, Pastor Im's heart almost broke.
And Satan would whisper, 'Where *is* your God? If there is a
God who answers a Christian's prayer, *why are you here?* Why
does He let you be so mistreated?'

"He could have listened to that tempter's voice. But, in the
midst of the tragedy overwhelming his country, he had no
room in his heart for bitterness. After he had prayed and was
strengthened, he said, 'Dear Lord Jesus, if You have let all
this heartache come to me and my family, it must be because
You have something for me to do. *What can I do* for You here
on this prison island?'

"He looked around at the other miserable wretches locked
away, many of them not knowing his God who answers prayer
and his Savior who loved them. His heart went out in pity.
Then one evening as the sun was going down, he did a bold
thing. He went around to six or eight of the men who he had
learned were Christians; men, who like himself, were North
Korean and thus suspect as enemies. 'Look,' he said to them,
'maybe God brought us to this place for such an hour as this.
Let's get together and sing the love of Jesus; let's sing some
Christmas carols.'

"So, forbidden though it was, this group gathered around

Pastor Im, right out in the open in the bitter cold and with the guns of guards and sentries pointed at them. Pastor Im stood on a wooden box and began to sing in Korean the carols the American missionaries had brought and taught. As they sang, 'Silent night, Holy night, All is calm; all is bright' other voices began to join in with them.

"The U.S. guards listened in amazement. Those were not Communist songs. They were tunes they knew even though they didn't understand the Korean words. Thinking it must be a trick, the guards aimed their guns toward the little group. But not one of them moved. They kept on singing carol after carol. Finally, the guards, not knowing what to do, sent for a high officer; but, before he could arrive, man after man stepped out of the tents and gathered around Pastor Im and the singers until there were nearly five hundred of them. The officer eyed the scene, called for the group to be dispersed by the guards, but something held the guards back. How do you break up a crowd that's just singing Christmas carols?

"They asked for the ringleader, and out stepped little Pastor Im who had now turned to a worn little Bible and was beginning to read the Christmas story. They waited until he had finished, then the guards broke up the gathering, and the prisoners walked to their tents. As they did, the officer said, 'There's something about this camp—there's a feeling I've never had before in a camp.' Some of the guards left with tears in their eyes.

"Pastor Im, leaving for his tent, put his hand on a man's shoulder as they walked. 'Friend,' he said, 'you who I don't know, but you're locked away here with me, do you know this Savior?' Pastor Im was busy doing personal work.

"The guards had called for Chaplain Voelkel, the American who understood Korean. When he heard Pastor Im's story, the chaplain arranged for Im to be given an armband that gave him permission to wander about and preach and hold prayer meetings every morning.

"Chaplain Voelkel joined him and, within a year, a miracle was happening on that island. Groups with as many as twelve hundred men were meeting in each of the compounds. They got up early to pray and to sing the gospel songs, especially 'Jesus Loves Me' and still had to be ready by six for inspection and review. Pastor Im and Harold Voelkel also held Bible classes inside the camp, and over six thousand men finished the six-month course of daily study and graduated.

"The wonderful, satisfying part is that now, long after the camps are closed and the men are free, six hundred of the prisoners have finished Bible School and Seminary outside Korea and are now back preaching the gospel—all because this one dedicated, fearless Christian, who was caught in deep personal tragedy during the bitterest hours of war in Korea. Instead of complaining, he turned to see what he could do to serve the Savior. Today he has a little church in South Korea. He has never learned one thing of what happened to his wife and family in North Korea. He just goes on serving Jesus."

It was men like Pastor Im that Dr. Bob had in mind when he spoke of heroes of the Cross, heroes other than the missionaries who need our prayers. Well he knew that it was not only the missionaries who merited our prayers and concerns, but also the brave nationals who took their stand for Christ.

Missionary to His Enemies

Dr. Bob had a firm conviction that God can bring good out of the worst evil. He often said that one of the fine outcomes of the war in the Pacific was that many G.I.'s who fought the Japanese in the defense of the islands returned as volunteers in Christ's service. He illustrated this for me with the following story:

"On 17 June 1945, the U.S. Marines were locked in a deadly struggle with the enemy over one of the last ridges of resistance on Okinawa. One of their tank corps was Lieutenant Bob Boardman. As he and his companions attempted to make it back to the field medical base with their wounded officers,

Japanese bullets slammed into Bob's neck and arms. He thought his time had come. But he was comforted knowing that he had recently settled the matter of his eternal salvation. Through reading a Gideon Bible, Bob had seen his need, confessed his sin, and received the forgiveness that prepares men for heaven. He had by faith accepted Jesus Christ as his Savior.

"Death was right there—but God had other plans. It took thirty-five operations, a year and a half in hospitals, but Bob was finally released (although he would wear a special tube in his neck for eighteen months).

" 'It's a miracle,' people said, for his wounds had been severe and critical.

"Then a greater miracle—the miracle of love—took place in the heart of this tall, Oregon State football-player-turned-Marine.

" 'How well I remember,' he told me, 'when God laid on my heart His call to the mission field. I said, "Yes, Lord, I'll go anywhere You want me to go." But as I pondered that commitment, I realized there was a reservation in my mind and heart. I was really saying, 'Yes, I'll go wherever You want me to go, dear Lord: anywhere, that is, *except Japan!*' "

"When I asked what influenced him to change from that determination, Bob Boardman always credited it to his hearing a testimony by Louis Zamperini, the former Olympic miler who came to know Christ in Los Angeles at the Washington Hill Street tent, when your father was preaching there in 1949. Captured, abused, and tortured by the Japanese, the Lord had given Louis the grace to witness to them of the love of Jesus Christ.

"This testimony spoke to the heart of the ex-Marine, and Bob Boardman gave himself without reservation to do the Lord's will, *anywhere*. Later, when he encountered Korean Christians who were still bitter toward the Japanese, he was able to help them overcome these feelings as he told them how the Lord had enabled him to forgive and to minister to the Japanese.

"There's a wonderful power in the world today that can

reverse the awful hate and hell of war—a force that is able to
heal the scars. I'm reminded of Romans 1:16, 'I am not
ashamed of the gospel of Christ: for it is the power of God unto
salvation to every one that believeth . . .' (KJV).

"But all the troubles of the world and the great struggles
between bitterness and hatred are not in Asia. Nor are the
enemies of hunger and cold and starvation restricted to Asia.
The great world-wide enemy of all mankind and the enemy of
God is Satan and sin. The crushing blows that mankind has
reeled under were born out of greed and lust—one man, one
nation, desiring to conquer another, and the same Satanic ele-
ment of sin is out to destroy America and the world. But there
is this wonderful power of the gospel of our Lord Jesus Christ
that is able to make these old wounds heal right and heal
cleanly. There is a power able to take any life anywhere and
salvage it, bless it, use it, transform it, make it what it ought to
be.

"This is what missionary Bob Boardman and others proved
as, putting behind them the hatred and bitterness, they made
their former enemies their target for Christian witness, and
ultimately many became their brothers in Christ. For with
God *nothing is impossible.*"

Tribute to a Contemporary

Like everyone else who has ever dreamed, thought,
planned, lived for missions, Dr. Bob revered the heroes of the
past: William Carey of India, Adoniram Judson of Burma,
Hudson Taylor of China, and David Livingstone of Africa. He
was especially inspired by these words by Livingstone:

Forbid that we should ever consider the holding of a commission
from the King of Kings a sacrifice, so long as other men esteem the
service of an earthly government as an honor. I am a missionary,
heart and soul. God himself had an only Son, and He was a missionary and a physician. A poor, poor imitation I am, or wish to be,
but in this service I hope to live. In it I wish to die. I still prefer
poverty and mission service to riches and ease. This is my choice.

At the same time, Dr. Bob had a hearty respect for contemporaries who were giving their all in missionary service. He never felt that missions had died when God took the great pioneers home. One man especially won Dr. Bob's high regard; and, when this man was suddenly called to meet the Lord whom he had been so faithfully serving, Dr. Bob wrote:

> A headline appeared in the news this past week, it read: "Dawson Trotman, Founder of Navigators, Drowned." But that didn't tell the story. Here was a man who first became concerned over the men aboard our battleships—men who often had very little spiritual help and encouragement. Dawson had the dedication it took to set about almost single-handed to do something about that, to provide help and a plan to strengthen young fellows who wanted to serve Christ even in military situations.
>
> Out of his concern came his commitment. He began by gathering a few men under his wing in his own home and emphasizing Scripture memorization. (He knew they couldn't always yank a New Testament out to share the gospel with a buddy, or to meet their own particular need.) He instituted a system using packets of small cards with selected Bible verses. These memory verse cards would fit anywhere. So, from this idea, Dawson Trotman spawned *The Navigators*, an organization that spans the globe. Today, the memory cards are a tool being used in universities for evangelism and as a follow-up in crusades and in one-to-one witnessing. With these cards we have trained men in Korea to be our follow-up teams, and we have used the Navigator memorizing in our orphanages. There's an untold host of people in this soul-rewarding business of memorizing Scripture—all because of Dawson Trotman of the Navigators.
>
> So, as my friend Daws suddenly stepped into heaven, he left a great vacancy—not only among his friends and colleagues in the Colorado Springs headquarters, but among his friends in the Billy Graham Evangelistic team and other groups committed to soul-winning and spiritual growth. He left a vacancy in the mission fields of Japan, Korea, Taiwan, Okinawa, the Philippines, India, and Europe, as well as in the States.
>
> We shed a tear at his absence from our midst for the moment, but rejoice that he is present with Christ in heaven.

God's Memorial Day

Each year we remember the heroes of our country who gave their lives in the wars. And it's right that we should. But if Dr. Bob were still with us, he would remind us on Memorial Day that there are other heroes—soldiers of the Cross, some lying in unmarked graves in the far places of the world, men and women who joyfully gave their all for Jesus Christ—these also must be remembered.

In his unique way he would tell us that the Bible doesn't speak of a Memorial Day, but it does tell us that God has a memorial book. Malachi, chapter 3, spells this out for us in verses 16 and 17:

> Then they that feared the Lord spake often one to another: and the Lord . . . heard it, and a book of remembrance was written before him for them that feared the Lord, and that thought upon his name. And they shall be mine, saith the Lord of hosts, in that day when I make up my jewels; and I will spare them, as a man spareth his own son that serveth him (KJV).

In my heart and mind I can hear Dr. Bob eloquently expanding on this theme.

"But not only does the Lord have a remembrance book, He has an *honor roll*. I think of times when I've stood in a foreign land where there's a plot of ground sacred to all Americans, for it commemorates our brave servicemen and women. There, carved in stone or marble, are the names, the honor roll, of those who died for their own country, or to purchase freedom for other oppressed peoples.

"God's honor roll is the eleventh chapter of Hebrews. There He records first the heroes noted for their outstanding faith, from *Abel* on through *Enoch, Noah, Abraham, Sarah, Isaac, Jacob, Joseph, Moses, Joshua*. Then the Bible account goes on to mention just *Gideon, Barak, Samson, Jephthah, David,* and *Samuel* by name, telling the exploits that give them their place in history.

"In verse 35, you'll find no names, just "others. . . .""

"For what are these unnamed noted?

"They were *tortured*, not accepting their release, in order that they might obtain a better resurrection.

"They were *mocked* and *scourged* . . . as was their Lord.

"They were *chained* and *imprisoned* . . . they were *killed with the sword* . . . they were *destitute* and *ill-treated* . . . they were *stoned to death* . . . they were *sawn in two*.

"The world was not worthy of such heroes—such is the Bible's summation."

So, as Dr. Bob would add, God has His Hall of Heroes, not only those who were put to the test for serving Him wholly and were afterwards delivered, but those who suffered trial and testing and gave their lives—casualties for Christ.

I need not tell you that martyrdom didn't end with the writing of the Book of Hebrews. Today, the Christian martyrs lie in hidden graves in Russia, China, Indochina, Africa, South America—wherever dauntless missionaries have ventured for Christ, not counting their lives dear unto themselves.

With few exceptions, no magazines wrote them up—there were no great spreads in *Life* or *Time* magazines and no bestseller written about them. They walked jungle trails, climbed mountains, crossed deserts and seas, and faced the attack of the enemy.

There are some this very hour, in the Muslim world, who, having confessed Jesus Christ and been baptized in His Name, have been ordered to renounce their new faith or be killed. They love Jesus Christ enough to be slain—*some by their own families*—because they will not acknowledge that Jesus is just *one* of the prophets they revere and not the *Son of God*.

Others have died (and some may yet die this year) in a concentration camp someplace on earth. It may have been eight or nine years ago that they were caught by the communists, and it may be that their families thought they were dead years ago. There was not the glamour of a publicized martyrdom; they were not stood against a wall someplace while friends and neighbors watched. No. They were picked up long years ago and arrested because of Jesus Christ and their faith in Him, and they've been dying someplace in obscurity. Dying by inches. Dying in loneliness. Dying in hardship. Dying of malnutrition. Dying without there being any great flash of inspiration about it. Just dying, that's all, because they loved Christ and would not deny Him.

Today, I'd like to give tribute to those who, having loved Jesus Christ and followed Him, were *not* delivered.

Gladly and joyfully they have given their own lives, their own health and strength, for the cause of Christ. But, for some, that was not the hardest thing they ever did for Him. They had to watch as their wives and their children were sacrificed—as loved ones were arrested, persecuted, and slaughtered before their eyes. Surely this was as great a test as was demanded of Abraham—greater, because Abraham had his son delivered back to him, safe. God spared that son.

The heroes I'm thinking of didn't have their children spared; they *died*. And today they lie in a grave in a foreign country somewhere.

But remember: God has not forgotten them. He has His remembrance book. And, He has said that one glorious day those in that book will be His jewels.

Hidden Heroism

Many of the true heroes of the faith are the *wives* of missionaries. Dr. Bob said, he could write a "big thick book" to validate that statement. But instead, I'll share a brief letter Bob received before his death. It is from the wife of a missionary in Ethiopia.

Did you ever wonder to yourself, "What is the matter with me anyway?" when everything seems to go wrong all at once? Lately it has been like that with us. There have been flat tires on the motorbike, and the car won't start unless you crank it like an old Model T Ford. Our tape recorder broke, and when my husband tried to fix it, he finished with some 'spare parts' and no idea where they went. Our clan Chief is laid up in bed because of the fall he and my husband had while on the motorbike. And there has been sickness. . . .

My husband was due home after a week-long trek. It was his birthday that day . . . but only the car and his dirty clothes arrived! A man completely unknown to me drove our car home and handed me a note. My husband was in the hospital with typhoid fever. What a way to spend your birthday!

Then trouble struck when our little girl came down with what we thought was mumps. But when her eye started to swell shut she was found to have an infection in her parathyroid gland. . . .

But all isn't bleak. Yesterday *four people received Christ as Saviour and destroyed their pagan fetishes.* Hallelujah, Bob! Pray for them . . . it's worth it all.

But *Why*, Lord?

Every now and then the world is shocked by a tragic story of violence on the mission field. In the days and weeks that follow any such incident, the same question always seems to arise. Why did God allow such a terrible thing to happen? Many people absolutely never grasp the answer to this question. But Dr. Bob did, and he answered it for me with this story:

In the spring of 1953 in northern Siam (the nation everybody now knows as Thailand) a gang of thieves were on their way to rob a rice mill. Instead they saw two foreigners on the outskirts of a small village. Believing all foreigners to be wealthy, they shot the couple down in cold blood in an effort to take from them their riches and goods. Little did the thieves realize how wealthy their victims were. They were richer by far than the robbers' greatest expectations, but the robbers could not lay hands upon *that* wealth. Only if they had let the foreigners live would they have known how to obtain such riches. For these foreigners were missionaries to Siam—missionaries who had heeded the words of Christ, "Don't store up treasures here on earth where they can erode away or may be stolen. Store them in heaven where they will never lose their value, and are safe from thieves" (Matt. 6:19–20, TLB).

All this thieving gang could take was the lives of Paul and Priscilla Johnson, missionaries of the Christian and Missionary Alliance Church.

Paul and Priscilla were holding a conference in their local church in a small village. I doubt if you can realize how dense is the forest, how rugged is the terrain of much of Thailand. There are still hundreds of villages way back beyond any motor roads, spots you can reach only on the back of an elephant (and there are many elephants still doing the work of tractors and trucks all over that rugged interior country).

Many Christians—humble little people of the villages—had come to spend a few days at the feet of their Christian teachers, Paul and Priscilla Johnson. The conference lasted for five days after Easter, and now it was Friday, April 18, the closing night. Priscilla was seated at the little reed organ. Paul, the leader of the meeting, was standing close beside her. The congregation was bowed in worship: Siamese Christians pray out loud.

In a house nearby, the Johnson's two children, Becky, age five and Billy, age two, were asleep; their seven-year-old brother, Brian, was safely attending the school for Missionary children in Dalat in Indochina. The beloved Siamese Christians began to close their prayer, and perhaps in Paul and Priscilla's hearts was an added note of thanks, for tonight was the eve of their first *furlough*. Time for rest and preparation before returning for another term.

Suddenly gunfire and a hail of bullets rang through the darkness. The missionaries were the target. Priscilla died instantly, slumping over the console of the organ. Paul dropped where he stood. Ten bandits then appeared from the darkness, warning the congregation to keep their heads bowed to the ground or they would be shot also. The greedy search for earthly treasures was a futile one. Ironically, the bandits didn't even get the jeep belonging to the Johnsons—for they didn't know how to release the emergency brake!

They entered the house, kicking aside the crying children as they rifled the missionaries' few possessions. Then returning to the road, they halted a passing truck, killed the driver in a fit of anger over their unprofitable raid, and drove off.

Shocked Christians rushed to the side of the missionaries. But there was no earthly help for Priscilla. Paul's reaction to the news of his wife's death, as he regained consciousness, was an expression of her glorious gain and the realization that Priscilla was now with the Lord. Then, in agony, Paul was moved to the city of Udorn, twenty miles away. There were several more journeys, mostly by plane, as the government of Thailand desperately attempted to aid in the saving of this missionary's life.

In the course of frequent suffering, he was heard to quote "the Lord giveth and the Lord taketh away, blessed be the name of the Lord." In the midst of frequent blood transfusions he sang over and over the chorus familiar to all Christian and Missionary Alliance folk—"Bless me, Lord, and make me a blessing. . . ."

While Paul's life hung in the balance, Thailand officials visited the scene of the tragic incident. They transported Priscilla's body to the city of Khan Kean for burial, and there on a Sunday morning they joined Siamese and Chinese Christians as the body of Siam's first missionary to meet violent death in the line of duty was laid to rest.

But Priscilla was not to be alone in heaven for long. The following Wednesday fellow missionaries scattered throughout Thailand received a brief telegram: "Beloved Paul gone to be with his Lord and his lovely Priscilla."

The story of Paul and Priscilla is, however, the story of a victory—not a tragedy. For they well knew that, whether they lived or died, they were the Lord's. Their treasure was in heaven. Paul and Priscilla were laboring to spread the news of the Savior's love, the Savior who died to free men from the penalty and power of sin.

The tragedy in our story is to be found in the many folks left behind who may have wept, who may have ached in pain, but who so often lived whatever life it was, good or bad, hard or easy, for nothing.

Even as Paul Johnson lay there on the stretcher in Udorn airfield, out of his suffering he said,

"May God forgive those who have killed my wife and wounded me. Lead them to a place of repentance, Lord. As for myself, I am ready to die. I have served Thee to the best of my strength and ability."

A Siamese newspaper reporter nearby heard those words, and throughout the kingdom, the incident became front-page news: "MISSIONARY PRAYS FOR BANDIT WHO KILLED HIS WIFE."

It's pretty difficult to ignore such a vibrant testimony as that, and their testimony did not go ignored.

Yes, Paul and Priscilla are gone. Courageous, capable Christian leaders aren't easily obtained for the world's frontiers of faith. *Why then did God permit these two to be martyred?*

Two things we are sure of, and the third thing we hope for. First, we know that because of their tragic death, all the missionaries in Thailand today enjoy greater protection and recognition than ever before.

Second, because of their exemplary sacrifice, the whole nation is more conscious of the sincerity and deep love true missionaries have for the Thai people.

What is the third result we hope for?—that God may use the example of Paul and Priscilla Johnson and their devotion to Christ which so moved Siam, *to move you to action.*

Dr. Bob had his own answer for the question, "Why, God?" It was this:

The heart of God breaks over every suffering, aching, lonely, hungry being on the globe—*God does care.* The great tragedy of earth isn't that *God* is indifferent, it's that *men* are indifferent.

To follow Christ may cost one his life. Jesus said so in the context of the man who set out to build a tower before sitting down and counting the cost (see Luke 14:26–33), or the kind who goes off to battle not having first reckoned whether he had enough men to finish the job. The Lord Jesus warned any who would follow Him to first count the cost. And in Luke 9:24 He says, *"Whosoever will save his life shall lose it; but whosoever will lose his life for my sake, the same shall save it."*

Young people interested in becoming missionaries need to know that some of our finest missionaries have been killed because of their witness for Christ, and the same thing could happen to them, too. And it may be that it won't be just their own life that is in danger—it may be a wife and children buried in some ungrassed plot in the rough old breast of Mother Earth.

I know it costs. It always costs. It always will cost. But remember (and this is so corny and hackneyed that I hesitate to say it, but there's nothing more true): "Just one life; 't will soon be past. Only what's done for Christ will last."

God knows why He took Paul and Priscilla Johnson to heaven by the martyr's route. There are no unanswered "why's" with God. And you who have just read the story about Paul and Priscilla could be one of His answers to "Why, God?"

9. David and Goliath
and the Generalissimo

EVERY PREACHER HAS what he calls his Royal George (a sermon he considers to be his best and which he trots out when he wants to impress people).

Dr. Bob Pierce was no different, but it can be said of him that in addition he certainly had some colorful listeners. One was Taiwan's General and President, Chiang Kai-shek, better known as the Generalissimo. Another thing about Dr. Bob was that he studied his audience. He was well aware that the Generalissimo, an avowed Christian, preferred Old Testament texts, especially as they related to war.

One day as we talked, Bob recalled the last time he preached for Chiang Kai-shek. His sermon was "The Day David Killed Goliath" from 1 Samuel 17. And it went like this:

Young David got up that morning, and he couldn't have known that it would be any different from all the other days. Being the youngest son, therefore a nothing in the family, he'd be stuck out in the wilderness with his father's sheep. That's the way his day would go, while his elder brothers were out in the thick of the battle with King Saul. But—along came his father and he sent David off with bread and ten cheeses for his brothers and instructions to bring back word of how they were doing.

So off David went, loaded down with food. When he reached the battle area several miles away, he approached someone in the

137

crowd and asked, "What's going on?" And with that his oldest brother pounced on him and spouted "What are *you* doing here?" Never a word of thanks for the bread and cheese the kid had hauled all that long way. "I know the naughtiness of your heart; you've come up here to see the battle"—as if there was something dreadful in a fellow wanting to see what was goin' on. He confronted David in front of everyone who was standing around, accusing him of leaving his legitimate job with the sheep: "What have you done with those few sheep in the wilderness that our father trusted you with?"

David answered him, "What have I done? I just obeyed my father and brought you this food, and I have to tell when I go back how it fares with my brothers."

Dr. Bob paused, then continued. "At that point, I digressed from the David story to remind my listeners that it often happens that way; the people who ought to love you the most and trust you are the very ones who will treat you the dirtiest. I was really preaching for the old General saying, 'Look, don't be surprised; that's the way it's been since the time of David.'

"Of course that really polished the apple with President Chiang Kai-shek because there were so many who were supposed to be helping him but were out to cut his throat. I had seen that during the three years I was in and out of Mainland China. Among other things, they would sabotage the money and supplies sent to help the Generalissimo, making them fall into the hands of the pro-Mao forces (I had been in places where I heard them brag about how they accomplished this.)"

Bob went on to say that he told President Chiang Kai-shek that there's a good ending to this story of David and his brothers:

It was actually *the abuse the brothers heaped on him,* especially the oldest one who should have been encouraging him and showing gratitude, that turned the onlookers in David's favor. Where this brother had intended to put him down and make a mockery of him and really destroy him in front of the crowd, *God caused it to backfire!*

These men who had witnessed the whole thing went and told King Saul all about the young guy who'd been so humiliated by his brothers after he had done them a good turn; how they had wrong-fully accused him of disobeying his father and neglecting his job—the whole bit. And they topped it by repeating to the King what David had said: "Why is that evil old giant out there allowed to say all these blasphemous things about our God? Why are you just standing here and nobody doing anything about it?"

They told the King all this, emphasizing, "This young fellow is somebody worthwhile; he's not like these brothers of his say he is. Moreover, *he's the only one around here who's not afraid of Goliath.*"

Can't you just imagine the conversation between the great King Saul and the little shepherd lad! I suppose at first the King was amused, but when he expressed his doubt that David could go against Goliath and succeed where his armies had failed, David had something to counter that! Can't you just hear him! Not proudly but confidently, young David tells the King how when a bear came and stole a lamb from the flock for which he was respon-sible, he went after it and slew it, saving the lamb, and the same when a lion threatened the sheep. "The Lord that delivered me from the paw of the lion and the bear," David told King Saul, "He will deliver me from the hand of this Philistine who dares to defy the armies of the living God."

No wonder the King was impressed!

"And then I went on to tell them the end of the story," Dr. Bob said, "how the boy David with his sling and his five stones—and his courage—killed the giant, Goliath!

"But, I reminded my audience in the Generalissimo's pri-vate chapel that day that it all began with a lad simply obeying his father, and going where his father sent him. It didn't prom-ise anything for David himself. He did it for his father who was concerned about his sons having enough to eat, and who was worried because he'd had no news from the battle zone as to how his sons were faring.

"I told them that David made no demands for himself. And that's *the one great difference* in life as to whom God uses to kill giants, and the ones He could never trust with the task because they'd be looking out for themselves.

"I didn't mean to preach a sample sermon," Dr. Bob said to me with a bit of a laugh, "but there you have it. I was getting around to how it affected the President of Taiwan that Sunday."

Dr. Bob didn't need to apologize to me. He's always so interesting that I had been all caught up in his sermon. But now I wanted to hear what had happened with President Chiang Kai-shek.

"Well," Dr. Bob said, "the Madame was sick that morning and couldn't be at the service, but there were twenty top generals as well as their chief who attended.

"About two o'clock in the afternoon, a runner came from the President's summer home and asked if I would please come for tea. The President's car picked me up in a few minutes, and I was soon at the Grass Hill residence. I was shown into Madame Chiang's room. She greeted me, then explained, 'Dr. Pierce, forgive me for asking you in these informal circumstances; but I do want to have *you* tell me what you preached this morning. You see, my husband came home this morning and went over first the Scripture you read as your text, then point by point *everything you preached.* And this is the first time he has ever come home and remembered the text and every point of a sermon.'

"She settled herself comfortably, called for tea, we prayed together, then I preached the David and Goliath story all over again.

"That was the last time I ever saw President Chiang Kaishek, Franklin. And I especially remember that occasion because, when I stopped to think of it, it was rather prophetic. I had preached for him before, and had been a guest in their home in Shanghai before the fall of China to Communism. Then he had invited me to preach five or six times when they first fled from the Mainland. But I felt that this sermon was prophetic in that here was this great man—maybe very small in other people's sight—'taking care of a few sheep out in the wilderness,' with the enemies of God blaspheming His name. But this godless crowd had better think twice, because they are not dealing just with little Taiwan.

"Though not an avowed Christian nation, that small country has, time and again, stood on the side of righteousness at the cost of its own interests. And the Communists may discover that our God still has His means of killing the Goliaths of earth on a day when nobody is expecting it. God can use a little Taiwan or any place else to slay a Goliath and change the course of history through someone who is just willing to obey Him as their Father, with no thought of their own interests."

10.   Here and There
with Bob Pierce

DR. BOB ONCE TOLD me that one of the highest compliments ever paid him was by Dr. Mackay, president of Princeton Theological Seminary. Shortly after the Korean War, Bob's films and broadcasts on the plight of Christians in Korea were attracting a lot of attention because the only thing people had been hearing about Korea in those days was the war news—nothing about what God was doing.

Bob Pierce at Princeton

Dr. Mackay invited Bob to the seminary for a two-day speaking engagement. He was to speak a number of times to the students. Bob explained it like this:

"I was given an hour each time with the entire student body present. And let me tell you, some of them were very critical of my grammar. And they had a right to be. As I keep telling people, I was one of those guys who skidded clear through eight years of grammar school, four years of high school, and almost four years of college (I dropped out and got married, but I took graduate courses at USC later) and never did learn basic grammar. Anyway, I mangled the king's English as I spoke to all those young intellectuals at Princeton who would go on to be leaders of the Presbyterian Church.

"Dr. Mackay had asked me to challenge the students to give their lives for the places in the world that needed them, instead of just being fed into churches and communities that would give them instant professional status.

"That was not a very popular philosophy at Princeton in those days. And the critics had a field day with me. But Dr. Mackay answered every critic with these words: 'Dr. Pierce has earned the right to be heard.'

"I count that *the highest compliment any human has ever paid me.* And it's my fervent prayer to God that some people will follow me and earn the right to be heard for Jesus Christ and the cause of missions."

International Ambassador

One Bible verse Dr. Bob took literally and personally is 2 Corinthians 5:20: "Now then we are ambassadors for Christ . . ." (KJV).

He believed that and lived by it. "An ambassador should act like an ambassador," he'd say, then add, "Since I am God's ambassador, I'm gonna expect Him to take care of me and my needs.

"If I have to sleep in the filth, I'll sleep in the filth—and I have. I've slept in the open jungle; I've slept with the bedbugs; I've slept surrounded by scorpions that would drop off the ceiling, in both China and Korea; I've eaten food that was unspeakable (like one of the early missionaries in Cambodia I've prayed, 'Lord, thank You for this food and please protect me from it'). But, on the other hand, I've also stayed in the finest hotels, eaten the finest food, and worn good clothes. The result has been that time and time again as I've gone to a mission field, I've met the president or the prime minister of that country, or the king or queen—whoever was in charge.

"A lot depends on your attitude: whether or not you recognize who you are in God's sight—what *He* has said you are.

"I just don't happen to believe that it's God's will for us to go around with nothing. He hasn't asked us all to take a vow of poverty in order to be good witnesses for Him. (In fact, it's worth pondering that historically most mission converts have come from the ranks of the poor. Is that because so few missionaries have walked in like ambassadors and witnessed to the equally lost rich, influential sinners?)

"If you feel your cause is number one, look like you think that's true. Hold your head up and walk in as though you have the most important job in the world to do—*which you have.*

"Of course, if you want to go around wearing cast-off clothing and feeling self-righteous—and like a nothing—you can. You can act like 'nothing' if you want to. *But don't pretend that God likes nothings as much as He likes somethings;* if God liked nothings, He'd have created a nothing. Instead He created *something,* and we have yet to fathom how great is that something.

"We need men and women who have this balanced attitude and conviction—people who are humble before God, who are aware that their power comes from His indwelling Holy Spirit, and who are confirmed in their mind that God has given them a high calling as His ambassadors.

"Paul never hung his head before any king but King Jesus. Remember his direct, candid, unashamed approach to King Agrippa? Here was a prisoner the Roman officials didn't know what to do with. When King Agrippa came to Caesarea for a visit, the Roman governor Festus unwittingly set up the chance of a lifetime for Paul when he told Agrippa about his unusual prisoner. Whether this king, who *knew* the Old Testament Scriptures, ever swung from being *almost* persuaded, we don't know. The fact is, King Agrippa got a chance to hear the gospel because Paul never lost sight of his God-given ambassadorship (Acts 26). He was always aware of the authority he had from Jesus Christ himself.

"Whatever authority I have God gave me; it wasn't something I was aware of, nor could I have given it a name. I just had no fear of walking into the office of a president or into the presence of a king or queen and saying, 'I'm Bob Pierce. God sent me, and I have a little business I want to talk over with you.' I don't remember a moment that I was ever aware I couldn't do that.

"I recall a time when I was in the midst of meetings in Seoul. The Lord was wonderfully blessing His Word as my fine interpreter, Dr. Hahn, translated my message into understandable Korean. At the same time an awful cloud of intense foreboding hovered over the crowds that kept building night after night. *Was this Seoul's last opportunity?* I kept asking myself.

"Then a phone call came from President Syngman Rhee, inviting me to meet with him in the Blue House (comparable to our White House).

"I remember being ushered into the house, then conducted through the large State and other formal rooms out to a sunny area of the garden. There on a small chair sat this 'George Washington' of his country: no man loved Korea or suffered for it more than he did. Next to him was another small chair for me.

"After the greetings, he said, 'Young man, tell me what you are here for,' and I shared with him my burden to see the young people of Korea come to a saving knowledge of Christ. We talked about the program, and I invited him to visit a meeting, even if he stayed in his limousine and listened over the public-address system. 'I would be honored, sir,' I told him.

"I can still see him—he was then over eighty, and he had first been tortured by the Japanese when he was eighteen. They had put sticks between each of his ten fingers and had broken every joint of each finger and thumb. He was constantly interlocking his fingers, rubbing some circulation into his hands; this was his most consistent gesture.

"'*You* are a Christian, Mr. President,' I said, for it was well known.

"He said, 'Yes, I gave my heart to Jesus when I was in prison, when I was eighteen years of age. There was nobody else around, and God awakened me early one morning and told me it was time to give my heart to Jesus.' (He had been educated at Padja High School, the great Methodist High School; and he had heard the gospel, but didn't believe until God woke him up in his prison cell that morning.)

"And, as we sat there, he said, 'What are you going to do about the *universities?*'

"I told him how our meetings went and I said, 'I have only so much strength, and Dr. Hahn, my interpreter, is an old man.'

"He said, 'You have a great man there.' He was pensive for a moment and then said, 'Dr. Pierce, if you want to win the young people of this country to Christ, you have less than two years to do it.'

"I said, 'What do you mean, sir?'

" 'I mean, if we don't have some kind of a spiritual renewal in this nation—if God doesn't do something to divinely intervene for us—the Communists are going to be sitting right here in this garden where you and I are sitting this afternoon.'

"(His words were all too prophetic, and they explained that ominous something we had all felt pervading the meetings. Within three weeks the Communists *had* taken over. President Rhee himself was fleeing a hundred and sixty miles to the nearest safe city. All the missionaries had gone. It *had* been Seoul's last chance.)

"But we didn't know that at the time. I promised the President I would do everything I could, explaining, 'I came because I'm staggered at the openness of your people right now to receive the gospel.'

" 'They are all afraid,' he answered. 'Every Christian knows he is a prime target, that just as the Communists killed the Christians in China so will they murder here. Our men in places of leadership in education, in legislature—practically all our leadership was trained in missionary schools. These are the first the Communists will attack; they are afraid of them, for the Christians have ideas and convictions and would stand up against the Communists. So our Christians are worried—and those who do not know Christ personally are searching for peace.'

"I listened to that grand old patriot and Christian brother, and what he said registered. I didn't know it then, but those nine weeks of ministry bound me with an everlasting tie to Korea, my beloved second home! How blessed they were to have as their President this man who read his Bible every day, who set an example to his nation by being in the front seat of a Korean church practically every Sunday of his life. And what a privilege it was for me to get to know him."

The Rain and the Train

I could tell that Dr. Bob had a lot more to say, and I listened eagerly as he continued.

"In my endeavor to carry out my promise to Syngman Rhee, the last city I preached in was *Inchon*. They had no stadium and no auditorium. We met outside in an open area that could accommodate twenty thousand right in front of the railway station. Everybody stood during the meetings. Elmer Kilbourne had an old jeep with no top, and we stood up in it with the PA system rigged up. But just *getting* to those meetings each night was something. The chuck holes on the one paved road were so deep they jarred loose not only every bolt on the jeep; they almost jarred my teeth out!

"Well, on our first night about twenty thousand came and, just as we started the song service, it began to rain. And, man, I mean *rain*. People around the edges immediately began to scatter. But I remembered something Dr. Charles E. Fuller had written about a meeting he had in a place that had a tin roof. The people were not getting wet, but the rain pelted so hard that the PA system couldn't make him heard. So he stopped everything, stood up, and asked God to just start turning off the faucet. The rain stopped. He preached his sermon. He gave his invitation and the people poured forward. They dealt with the people and then as they started out of the auditorium, boy, the heavens let loose!

"So, here I was in the same situation and scared to death to try that kind of a prayer in front of twenty thousand people. What if God didn't *do* it? So, I stood up there and asked all the people to be quiet. Then I said, 'Our God is the true and living God. With Him all things are possible and He has promised,

'You can say to this mountain, be removed, and it shall be moved and with that nothing shall be impossible.' That's hard for me to believe and I'm scared to death to put it to the test, but I don't want you people running away right now. *You wait to see God do a miracle.*' Some people were already five hundred yards away, but my PA system was loud enough that it stopped them. And I just said:

> God, you know how long we've waited for these meetings, and we have only this week; this is the last chance I have to preach Jesus to these people. We don't know how much longer Korea has and the saints have prayed for this night and sacrificed and worked. You know that we're here to do Your will and to preach Your Son's gospel. We don't want anything else but Your will. Now, I ask You, because You said with us nothing shall be impossible, I ask You to stop this rain right now.

"And it stopped! They streamed back, and the next night everybody was hoping that there'd be another rainstorm or something. Everybody likes miracles.

"The next night we had a fairly peaceful meeting. No rains. No disturbance. Everything was fine. We had set the time for the meetings at an hour when the trains were all gone for the day. There were no rattling box cars or any streaking locomotives or anything else. Well, on the third night when I was about four minutes into my sermon, suddenly . . . choo, choo, choo . . . here comes an engine without a car of any kind behind it. Just a big locomotive engine and the engineer pulled in right alongside the station, directly dead center to this platform of ours with the crowd gathered all around it. Suddenly the engineer pulled the whistle rope. He'd pull it and hold it down for two or three seconds, then let it up; then he'd pull it down and hold it and let it *shriek!* When it did, of course, you couldn't hear a thing. He'd let me start to say something and the minute my interpreter, Dr. Kim, started—shriek went that whistle!—till it was getting on all our nerves. I thought that maybe it had to do with a train he was trying to signal and then he would move on, so we waited about ten minutes.

"Most of the people still were waiting to see what I was gonna do. This time they weren't running off as they did in the rain, because they weren't getting wet. But their ears were hurting and they were waiting to see what we'd do next.

"I'm not very patient, so I said inwardly to the Lord, '*What are you doing, ruining everything? I really don't understand this. I thank you for the miracle of stopping the rain the other night and I want to praise You for it, but this is just devastating. It's going to ruin the meeting. People are going to leave in just a few minutes, and I don't know whether they'll ever come back because it begins to be apparent that this is a deliberate act by Satan. Some man who is either a Communist or hates Jesus Christ has gotten hold of this engine and pulled it in here deliberately to destroy this meeting.*'

"I called Dr. Kim and two or three elders of the different churches and asked, 'What shall we do?'

"They looked at each other and at me, hesitated a little, and then one spoke up, 'If God could stop the rain for us, why can't God move this engine away?'

"I should have answered, 'Yes, if God can do that for us once so that people can hear His Word and be saved, he can do it a *thousand* times.' But I have to admit, I didn't have that much faith. However, there was no alternative.

"So, in a brief lull, I stood up in front of that audience and I challenged the devil:

I command you, Satan, in the name of Jesus Christ, to still that shrieking whistle and to get that man and his engine out of here *at once*, so that people who have never heard the gospel will hear and be saved. And I thank You, Lord, for defeating Satan and I ask You in the name of Christ to command these demons and whoever they are who have brought this engine and disrupted this meeting to move it out of here and still that thing *this very second.*

And that very second the wheels began to move and that train backed off clear out of sight and sound, and we never had another peep out of it for the rest of the seven days of the meetings.

"Now that may sound as if I am bragging, but God knows I was never more sincere. I had nothing to do with it. I just believe that Jesus is so faithful that only He could have given me the faith those nights. And the results were two absolute miracles in front of twenty thousand people in two out of three days. Even Elmer Kilbourne told me he had never seen a more demonstrable step of faith. It was an electrifying thing to him; and, after that whenever I preached, we had an audience who would believe *anything we told them about Jesus;* and the results were fantastic because miracles *had* been performed and everybody knew it!

"Most places I've been, I've hesitated to tell these stories because they strain the credulity of most people. So those true incidents are probably two of the least told of the great miracles God has wrought in my life.

"But Bob Finley and Elmer Kilbourne and Dr. Kim and all the others who were there saw them happen; and, sitting in my Hollywood apartment on January 1, 1978, Elmer Kilbourne confirmed them once again. And we praised the Lord together all over again for His great faithfulness."

Madame Chiang Kai-shek's Question

Turning his attention once again to the subject of being an ambassador for God, Dr. Bob recalled his first meeting with Madame Chiang Kai-shek:

"On my first trip to China, I had a reason to see President Chiang Kai-shek. I just called up his office and said, 'I am here from one of the largest Christian youth organizations in America, and I have the Bible that was given to me to present to the president on behalf of these Christian young people.'

"Well, he was away, but Madame sent for me and I went to her home and sat in her front room on a hot, sweaty afternoon in Shanghai. I remember it was so hot, and I sweat so much. . . .

"I told her what I was doing in her country. She didn't give a rip in that situation about whether anybody became a Christian or not. She said, "What you *ought* to be doing is getting some playgrounds and equipment for these little children on these crowded streets. Buy some land and get them some playthings so that these kids who are being crushed in the streets with traffic would have a little place to play.' That was her first remark to me. I replied, 'I *do* care about that, and I will do it if you think we ought to—if that will help me make an opening so that they can come to know how much Jesus loves them.'

"She said, 'You know I am a Christian. I write it. I speak it in public; but I care about these other things, too.'

"'Well,' I said, '*I* care about them, but I care about them *second.*' I remember that was our first conversation, but that was the beginning of a friendship that later caused her to send for me in Taiwan.

"It was Sunday, June 15, 1950—and I'll never forget it.

"I went at her request and she said to me, 'Why are you not sending missionaries to us here in Taiwan where we guarantee you religious freedom? We welcome Bibles. I wish you would send a hundred thousand—a *million* Bibles in here. Send or bring Bibles in Chinese or, what has been the language of this country for four hundred years, Fukinese.

"Then she asked, 'Who is truly concerned about winning the Chinese to Christ? I want to know *who is going to do anything* about it?'

"'I will,' I promised, and with this commitment heavy on my heart I flew home and a week later preached at Winona Lake; first for the Oriental Missionary Society and then for Youth for Christ. After talking about the Korean tragedy, I took off on Madame Chiang Kai-shek's fervent appeal and concluded with this invitation:

> All of you here tonight have a right to be *insurance people, school teachers, plumbers* or *musicians*—anything you want to be—after you have become a Christian. But not until, you've offered your body a living sacrifice to God, having been saved and having heard Christ say, 'Go ye into all the world and preach the gospel to every creature.' I mean by that the interruption of your plans—even your engagement if need be or your present course of university studies—everything under the sun so that you can become a true

follower and disciple of Jesus Christ Who said, 'If any man will
come after me, let him deny himself, and take up his cross, and
follow me.'

"I remember I added, 'More than likely, God will not pick
one out of a hundred of you here tonight. I doubt that He'll call
one out of a thousand. And if you're not called you're not to go.
But not one of you has a right to be anything else—once you're
a true believer—until you have made the offer to go, until you
have made sure that *God is not calling you*. If God says, "I
haven't chosen that for you; I've chosen for you to be a doctor or
a nurse here in your own land—I've chosen you to be a truck
driver or a whatever," at that point you have the right to be
anything at all that God tells you to be and that your heart
desires.'

"Someone said that my sermon that night had hit like a
sledgehammer blow right between the eyes. It hit so hard that
the people staggered out of the Billy Sunday Tabernacle with a
headache that lasted the rest of the night.

"Maybe so. Two men God spoke to that night are *Dick Hillis*
and *Ellsworth Culver*, both of whom have been a power for
Jesus Christ in Asia and are still serving Him to the hilt today.

"Coming back to the 'ambassador' subject: looking back, I
can recognize that it was this God-given authority to 'stand
before kings for Christ's sake' that opened doors of opportunity
for me to minister and to have a part in responding to pleas
such as Madame Chiang Kai-shek's.

"It was always a bit of a conundrum to me that so many
missionaries (fine men and women, better educated, more
experienced, more qualified in many ways than I am)—people
with a passion to win others to Christ—would for some unknown reason neglect this avenue toward reaching the influential lost nationals. Yet these nationals are the very people who
many times hold in their hands the power to open or close the
door to the missionary.

"I wasn't in Vietnam two weeks until I went to see the
president. We became friends. I've done this with Queen

Wilhelmina, with President Syngman Rhee, with President Chiang Kai-shek, and countless others.

"In fact, the reason I wasn't captured in Korea when the war began was that I had left on the Friday before to preach for President Chiang Kai-shek in his private chapel on Sunday. The war broke out that Sunday. The seven men I had been with in Korea were caught when the invasion came. Harold Voelkel had driven me to the plane. The other seven men were captured and made the long walk into North Korea; and it was two and a half years before they got out by way of a trade, through Moscow. I could have been captured, but instead God got me out with fifteen thousand feet of color motion pictures of the very town where the invasion from North Korea into South Korea was made. We'd been having a kind of little retreat there at a school.

"Dr. Christy Wilson reminded me of an experience we'd had together once in Iran. (Christy is that intrepid man who was the last pastor of the Protestant Church in Kabul, Afghanistan, before the Afghan government tore it down, undoubtedly one of the finest and bravest men I know). Well, he and I were together in Iran, and we went to see the minister of foreign affairs. He was away seeing the Shah someplace on the Caspian. The Secretary said, 'The minister is not here; would you care to see the deputy minister?' Christy has said he would never forget my answer, 'No, thank you, we want to see the *minister*,' and he told me it taught him a lesson. The minister of foreign affairs is the one who would have made the decision on the matter we wanted to see him about. Why short-circuit our chances? To see the deputy minister would have meant just being stalled—or downright *refused*. We waited there in Tehran until the minister of foreign affairs returned. I saw him and he granted me permission to bring the Korean Orphans' Choir to Iran. [This children's choir, started by Dr. Bob, became world renowned. They were his pride and joy and brought great inspiration wherever they sang.] We were given their Red Lion Orphanage to house the children and one of the main auditoriums in Tehran for our concerts. Officially (though she did not come to the concerts herself), the Empress was our sponsor.

"The point I'm making in all this is: If you are an ambassador, *act like one.* We have the highest calling on Earth. As ambassadors we carry with us the greatest word for all nations. Talk about diplomacy! We carry with us the *message of reconciliation,* to people who will never know peace without it! And there's something about ambassadors: they're not promoting themselves; they are to convey the message from their king or president or whoever sent them. Likewise, our King relies on us to convey His message.

"Somehow the Lord never let me wait for anybody to instruct me. I never thought about how you do it. I just picked up a phone. I met kings and queens because it is so *simple!* I didn't have brains enough to know that you couldn't do it—and this sort of thing has happened to me all my life.

"God tells me something, and I start on some cause. Oh, I know I'm going to be responsible, I am going to share the pain, or the shame if it boomerangs, as it sometimes has (maybe I was too hasty or misread God's directions). But that's what my life has been ever since I asked the Lord to break my heart with the things that break His heart.

"I have sinned, drifted away, rebelled against God—gone through all kinds of things—but there's that old fish hook! God only has to yank the string and there I come! That is one of the greatest things that could ever have happened to anybody—to let God put a fish hook into you so deep that there is no way of ever getting off the hook. And, somehow, along the way, the Lord has allowed me to be, to some degree, one of His ambassadors.

"With this conviction has come the driving urge of '*This one thing I do.*'"

Pat Robertson's Questions on the 700 Club

In a return appearance on the 700 Club, after Dr. Bob had thanked the television and studio audience for their prayers and financial support and reported how this had helped in evacuating over a thousand Vietnamese during the previous three days, the following discussion took place between Dr. Bob and Pat Robertson:

PAT: You've seen so much suffering, Bob. And I know that you once asked God to break your heart with the things that break His heart. This has been a challenge to many of us who've heard you say it. Now, I'd like to ask: How does it feel to you *now* to have said that? And what challenge do you have for us today?

BOB: Before the program I was talking with one of your associates as to whether missions is kinda going out of style. What is God doing today, and can young people do something now, world-wide, to bring men to Christ?

As I told him, a man can no longer go out into a totally alien culture—say China, or India, or the Muslim world—and build a little papacy with himself as Pope; he cannot say to the nationals ("natives" as some insensitive people still call them), "You do this and so." What it costs in these days is a kind of consecration that makes you willing to go and *not* be Pope or bishop or boss, but to be *literally* the servant.

It's humiliating to have to subjugate your knowledge, your experience, and especially that something we Americans are scarcely conscious of—our *status*. We're status crazy!

PAT: You're probably right about that, Bob!

BOB: Yes, and that's part of the real Cross . . . to serve Christ where you are most needed, in some parts of the world where the gospel has never once been preached. Someone has to go and pay that humiliating price of literally letting your ego be stomped on—not just pushed in and suppressed, but laid out there for people to stomp on. We need to do this by the grace of God with love and patience: sow the seed on rocky soil, nurture it, and maybe never be applauded.

PAT: That kind of goes against the grain for most of us. But, of course, you're right.

BOB: And that's the kind of dedication that is harder to find than money to build big institutions. But it's what God is really

looking for—not so much money. He's got that if He wants it.
Not technical equipment. He can get that any old place He
wants. The hard thing now is to find the person who will pay
that price in personal commitment to Jesus Christ. So now,
Pat, my friend, I come back to your first question: How does it
feel to have said to the Lord, "Let my heart be broken with the
things that break Your heart."

PAT: Yes. Let's talk about that.

BOB: I'm almost home, Pat. It won't be long now until I'll be
with Jesus—unless, that is, He intervenes.

Am I sorry that I told the Lord to let my heart be broken? I
want to tell you this, Pat: He did break my heart. He has many
times. I lost a beautiful daughter as part of the price of serving
the Lord. It cost my wife enormously: it cost her a lifetime of
loneliness while I was ten thousand miles away. It takes a toll
on your loved ones. But God takes care of that. And, after all,
Christ did say, to anyone who wants to serve Him in key spots
that will make a difference in history, that we have to be willing
to give up those we love the most on earth. But He also promised us we would reap everlasting life and a hundred-fold in
this life.

I have to testify to two things, Pat: Commit yourself, give
yourself away to God irrevocably, forever. Say to Him, "Go
ahead and burn me up. Spend me. Eat me up. Use me for your
glory"—and He will take you at your word! And *it will cost.*

PAT: And the second thing? The other side of it?

BOB: The other side is: What about all the guys who're working for IBM or General Motors or on the Stock Exchange—or
selling vacuum cleaners? It costs just as much *not* to serve the
Lord. And there's no added reward of the joy that comes
through wholly serving Him; no assurance that your life is
having eternal significance. It's wonderful to serve Jesus. I tell
you the fringe benefits, the little things you don't expect are so
exciting and glorious. God won't be anybody's debtor. Whatever you give up for Him, He's going to pour back double dips
and more.

PAT: You have so many friends in heaven right now you

won't know what to do with them all. You've just returned from Vietnam. You didn't have an inkling that you had leukemia?

BOB: No, none whatever. Some time back I picked up amoebic dysentery in India. This affected my liver so that it had to be operated on. So I just thought that the abdominal pain was due to a recurrence. I went to the hospital just for that. Then the minute they checked my blood count, the doctors knew and they went into a panic. A dear doctor friend of mine at Scripps Clinic in La Jolla (near San Diego) had a bone marrow study done. This confirmed that I have what is called chronic granularcytic leukemia. Ordinarily, this means you have about two years to live. I told the doctor, "Just tell me the truth. If this is it, I'm all ready; for heaven isn't something I'm trying to put off.

PAT: Well, you know the Bible says, "Precious in the sight of the Lord is the death of His saints." Although I am not sure it's time to take you out of here. There's an awful lot left to do.

BOB: I believe there is. But I have to be careful how I say I have a lot of things to do yet. However, we've just been able to make inroads to a tiny kingdom 'way up in the mountains between China and India: *Bhutan.* There wasn't even a road in there till last year; we've never been permitted to have even a medical missionary there. Now the king has given his permission for one of our wonderful, spirit-filled nurses, a British girl we've worked with in Afghanistan, to go in and work with the leprosy afflicted. I'm going to visit her. I leave Sunday, God willing.

PAT: And what does your doctor say to that?

BOB: Oh, "If you really take care of yourself, you can maybe last two years." I said, "But, Doc, I don't want to *last!* I got the lasting part when I accepted Jesus. I have *ever*lasting life. It's just a question of how long I'll walk on this tiny planet instead of walking through the universe with my Lord."

God can heal me; and I'm ready to have Him heal me, but I'm not going to ask Him to. Some dear godly souls are saying, "I'm going to pray you will be here another thirty years." And I'm telling them, "Please don't pray that. I might miss the

Rapture! I don't want to stay here twenty years if Jesus is coming in six months. Just leave it to the Lord. Oh, how wonderful to belong to Jesus!"

PAT: The joy of it! We live for the Lord and, even whether we live or die, we are the Lord's. It doesn't matter. Isn't it glorious! Knowing this buoys you up regardless.

BOB: "Why would you think of going to *Bhutan?*" my doctor asks, "You know it's loaded with infection. You can't get pure water to drink—"

"Why am I going?" I said, "I'm going because I don't want to go to heaven from some modern hospital. I would rather have three active months serving the Lord than have two years lying someplace wishing I was someplace else. You say it's a considered risk. Except, as far as I am concerned, there isn't any risk. The worst that can happen to me is the *best*—I would go to heaven.

PAT: That's right. And the "worst," I guess, is that the Lord will heal you! So you win either way.

BOB: Now I must be honest with you, Pat. I'm not wanting to sit by and say, "Okay, Lord, let me suffer a lot of pain from cancer." I'm not praying for trouble, I assure you. And now that I can look back on my life as I've tried to live it for the Lord, I don't know but that it would be harder for me today to pray that prayer, "Lord, let my heart be broken. . . ." Today I might think more about it because I know what that heartbreak means. I know a little more about what it costs.

PAT: We'll be praying for *God's will* for you, Bob.

BOB: What I want to bear testimony to is that no matter what happens, all my life up to this moment is the living testimony of God's faithfulness, not mine, because God knows the sins that are under the Blood, and in the midst of all my trying to serve the Lord, the failures! Thank God my friends don't advertise my sins with tributes on film. God covers them, and the story of my life is really the story of how God, in spite of me, did certain things because He wanted to do *His will*.

But I want everyone listening to us to know one thing for

sure, and that is, though they may have a terminal illness as I have, they can have absolute peace. They aren't an accident. They are in the hands of God. I feel so good about that I can hardly stand it, and I am ready to go to heaven right from here! I am also excited to be *alive* at this moment, and the only reason I would hesitate to rush off into the presence of Jesus is that I would hate to miss anything that is yet to go on.

The ABC's Gospel Schools

Anyone close to Dr. Bob has heard him refer to Korea as "my beloved second home." It figures, then, that in recording material for a book to be written after he would no longer be with us, he would include stories about the Korean children for whom he gladly gave years of his life. It never failed to disturb him when a *child* was deprived.

"If ever you want to see a heart-tugging picture," he would say, "you ought to go and watch a group of little Korean kiddies at school where there isn't a single pencil—no blackboard—no writing paper! Often, in the cold of winter, if there's a bit of sun they'd sit outdoors and write their lessons on the only thing they could afford to write on—the *dirt*, the ground. I've watched them as with a sharpened twig they'd form their characters and do simple addition and subtraction."

But all that changed because of one man, a man with both heart and vision like himself, Dr. Francis Kinsler, veteran Presbyterian missionary. He and Dr. Bob became close friends. When Dr. Bob recalled the story about the ABC's Gospel Schools, he said:

"At that time, there were almost no free schools in Korea, even on the lower grade level. There's an explanation for this: first, it has not been the custom in Asiatic countries to offer free education; then the wars destroyed what schools there were in Korea. About the only schools available were far too costly for parents who had lost everything; they just could not afford to send their children.

"It grieved the kindly Dr. Kinsler to see these many, many Presbyterian churches all over Korea being used just for Sunday services, sitting idle through the week.

"'Why don't we make them more useful by turning them into day schools?' he asked. 'And we could also take some of the fine Christian women whose husbands were killed in the war and give them a job teaching these little ones.'

"There were innumerable children living all around those churches; some attended, but by far the most did not. Maybe their parents who wouldn't let them come to a church service would be glad enough to let them come to learn the ABC's.

"Do you know what happened as a result of just that one man's caring and then acting upon it? By 1957, in the Presbyterian churches alone, seventy-two thousand little children were going to school for half days, six times a week! And other churches had caught on and were also utilizing their worship facilities during the week to teach neighborhood children. And what a ministry for the widows! Some had high school educations; some, Bible school training; all gave themselves to teach little children who, otherwise, would have grown up without the ability to read and write.

"Naturally, these schools were a marvelous gospel opportunity. The children were taught to sing and I've heard as many as twelve thousand of them at one time sing for us at a get-together in Seoul. How they would sing! Especially: *Jesus loves me; this I know, For the Bible tells me so.* Among other things, they learned *to read from the Bible.*

"So the children are learning—both Christian and non-Christian—while by serving in His Name the Christian teachers are proving to those around that Jesus does care, that He cares about *all* children.

"'I think,' said Dr. Kinsler, 'that this is one of the greatest ministries we can have. The far-reaching development is that in these schools, little Bible Clubs have sprung up.' (The Bible Club movement is strong in Korea today.)

"And, because so many of the children and their parents have been influenced by the gospel through these schools and the love evidenced there, they are getting behind this Christian educational effort to make it a permanent part of the church and secular life of their villages and towns. So a project that was begun as a stop gap by Dr. Kinsler, because there was no other way to do anything about the problem, worked out so that the people themselves want permanent Christian schools."

Dr. Bob continued, "Now here was a man who, on the one hand, wrote the *Systematic Theology* for the Korean church (a brain among brains) and on the other hand just couldn't stand by to see a kid with nothing but a twig to write with. He just had to get these children indoors, persuade pastors to let the kids sit in the church—even if they did mess it up a bit—and get an education. Do you know what this makes me think of, Franklin," he said, "so many of us do *nothing* because we can't do *everything*. Fran Kinsler couldn't give all the children in Korea a grammar school education; so he did what he could do. And, before he knew it, there were seventy-two thousand children being taught. It may not be up to our standards in America, but hardly anything in war-ravaged Korea was up to our standards. Still, it's amazing what you can do if you're sufficiently moved by someone else's needs. If you're not, it wouldn't matter if you had all the tools and know-how. Someone asked one of my friends in Korea, 'What did you do to become a missionary? What kind of a call did you have? How do you *know* you have a call to be a missionary?'

"My friend said, 'Look, I don't pretend to say that I'm equal to the opportunity or that I'm adequate for the need. I'm just *available*.'

"That's the kind of man Fran Kinsler is—available to take on one more task because it needs to be done. That's the kind of man, Franklin, that God's always looking for and has a hard time finding at times. And that's the story of the ABC's Daily Gospel Schools."

"But knowing you, Dr. Bob," I said, "you didn't just feel bad and wring your hands and tell Dr. Kinsler you'd pray for him. How did you become a part of these ABC's Schools?"

"Well, you're right. That picture was indelibly printed on my mind—the little kids struggling to learn and no tools or a thing to help them write their lessons (in those countries they use slates); so, at first, we began to send five hundred dollars a month for equipment, which was a lot of money in those days. We met other needs as they arose, and every time I was in the area I would stop and visit the schools and check out what we could do for them."

Years have passed, and now some of these children Dr. Bob once helped are pastors and evangelists; some Bible Club movement leaders (Jeanette tells me she has had some in her writing workshops as they're learning to write their own material).

And now we'll move on with Bob Pierce to another area.

When God Butted in—
Missions Versus Chemistry

People have asked me, "Franklin, what motivated you to get into missionary work?" The Annoor Hospital in Mafraq, Jordan, is where I got my vision for missions. When I was eighteen years old, I heard about this particular hospital and the need they had for an automobile. The Palestine Liberation Organization (PLO) had stolen the missionaries' car. Until then, my understanding of missions was only what I observed when missionaries came home on furlough: if narrow lapels were in style, they had the wide lapels; if narrow ties were in style, they had the wide ties; if they told jokes, they were always jokes that had been told four years earlier. That was my impression of missionaries—people who were always out of style.

But when I discovered that these missionaries in Jordan were on foot, having to walk while at the same time they were trying to build a hospital out in the desert (a hospital which would provide them a lot more room and, of course, one that would isolate the people with TB from the townsfolk), I was determined to help raise money for a car, and I did. When I drove the car out to Mafraq to present it, I was invited to do some construction work. They said, "We can't pay you anything, but we can feed you." I was challenged by the need and decided to stay.

Over the years I would go back to do construction work, and I also helped raise money for them. This is actually how I met Dr. Bob Pierce. Meeting with him for the first time in Atlanta, I shared with him the work at Mafraq and asked if he would be willing to help. He said nothing and went on. Two days later he called me to say that he wanted to go out to Jordan to meet these people—Dr. Eleanor Soltau, Lester Gates, Dr. Wes Ulrich, and the chief of nursing, Miss Aileen Coleman. Dr. Eleanor Soltau, I found out later, had gone to school with my mother in North Korea. Eleanor's father was a Presbyterian missionary there. Lester Gates was a retired farmer whose wife had died several years earlier. All he had ever done was farm; but now he was out there in the middle of the desert building this beautiful hospital. Dr. Ulrich was from Nebraska and the newest man to join the medical staff. Aileen Coleman had been kind of a renegade nurse in Australia, a woman who had at one time in her life rebelled, yet God got a hold of her and called her all the way to the Middle East to minister to these Bedouin people.

I discovered that these missionaries were not out of style at all, but were serving God at great personal sacrifice. I had been judging all missionaries by their outward appearance, but God looks at one's heart. Once when Dr. Bob met with these men and women in a small, unfurnished room at Annoor Hospital, the following dialog took place:

BOB: Dr. Wes Ulrich is a glorious example of how God sovereignly butts into a life. I say "butts"—*interferes* is too gentle a word for it. At times God just butts in and totally disrupts what has been up to then a life filled with disciplined planning, preparation, and precise direction. He just skids everything to a halt—and takes over. It isn't a way we like, nor something we would ever choose; and it can be both confusing and painful. I'm talking to a man who knows all about this. Yet here he is . . . *radiant!* 'Way out here among the Bedouins, working just thirty kilometers from the Syrian border where fireworks are common at night as the Israelis and Arabs bomb each other. Syrian raiders even crossed the border and stole all the hospital vehicles. But that's not what I want to talk about right now. I want Wes to tell you something of how God yanked him here, and I may not even butt in, at least not much!"

Wes: Well, first, I'm thirty-two, and as Dr. Pierce said, I grew up in Nebraska among the cornfields. Both my parents were believers, and my twin brother and I came to know the Lord. I remember that even as a youngster I had an interest in missions. But *chemistry* was a dominant part of even my early life. I wanted to be an analytic chemist. So the two—missions and chemistry—were competing in my mind. This later led to my undoing, for I felt there was no place in missions for analytic chemistry. Along the way, in high school, I decided to go into medicine with my brother.

Through an aunt who knew about Houghton College's fine science program, I went back to New York and got my chemistry degree at Houghton. There I met the finest college teacher I've ever known. The good experience I had at Houghton was largely due to him.

Bob: I know Houghton. Its great president, Dr. Stephen Payne, is a good friend of mine. So you're still on target, Wes. Houghton didn't dull your vision for missions. So . . . ?

Wes: From there I went to the University of Chicago Medical School. I'm not blaming the school, but that's where my undoing started. I began to seriously doubt this relationship I had with God. I couldn't feel it—I couldn't see it—I couldn't hear it; it just *wasn't real.* All these tangible aspects of faith were gone. At the time, of course, I didn't realize the folly of such reasoning. I had set aside the truth that the things that are seen are not of faith; that either you believe in the Lord Jesus, "Whom not having seen, you love"—or you *don't.* It's that simple. Well, after carrying on under terrific inner struggle, I finally concluded that God, in Christ, was simply not real in my life, and *finished*. I threw it all overboard.

BOB: Just like that.

WES: Just like that, Dr. Pierce.

BOB: Then what?

WES: Then is when—as you put it—God butted in.

BOB: You mean God just said, "Wes, I understand. I know med school is rough and you're a bit mixed up." And you went on as usual.

WES: No, sir! Things really changed. Suddenly *I* was responsible. Where before I would blame Satan for the bad things that came into my life and thank God for the good things, now it was *my* life. I was responsible for my own life. That meant that whatever I did with my life had to be valuable. It became increasingly clear that the menial tasks of life simply weren't valuable. I began to think more and more that the creative elements such as I'd find in engineering were *ultimately* valuable. I began to disregard more and more the fact that medicine really helped that much. Oh, I admitted that it brought somebody back to a state of health, but since it all ended in death anyway it didn't really matter. This began to affect my personal life, and in time I changed directions from medicine and got into engineering.

BOB: You found that satisfying?

WES: At first, yes. I thought I had really hit it. But I soon realized that at the same time life was becoming more and more difficult.

BOB: How? In what ways?

WES: It's kind of hard to explain, Dr. Pierce. I'd get up in the morning and couldn't convince myself that anything was really worth all the effort—that life itself was worthwhile, in spite of the fact that I was doing well in my studies, engineering and medicine. I was working at setting up an outpatient department in geriatrics in Minneapolis—all this *should* have satisfied me. . . .

BOB: So what was the problem?

WES: My life was increasingly empty. I'd actually have to

remind myself who I was and what I was doing. I was beginning to lose my orientation. Well, after enough crises, one afternoon—I remember it well—I just said, "Lord, I can't go on this way. My life is a wreck from the inside out. If you can give me a real purpose in life, *fine*." It was a bitter pill because I didn't really want God, didn't want His plan for my life. But it wasn't a matter of whether I wanted it or not; it was a matter of whether I would take it.

I said, "Okay, Lord, you can have my will; I will be obedient even though I just don't like what I know is coming." And gradually my orientation returned; and, instead of being overwhelmed with a sense of trying to find purpose in living, my life became completely filled with the purpose Christ had for me. He had died for me, He had saved me from my sins, and His purpose for me seemed to lean toward the mission field.

BOB: That certainly must have changed some things. How did you know which way to go, Wes?

WES: I certainly didn't know, until I was working in the Naval Medical Research Institute on decompression sickness. Then—I guess you'd call it God butting in—my aunt suggested I have dinner with Dr. Stanley Soltau.

BOB: I knew him well as one of the most loved missionaries in all of Korea. I think I know what's coming.

WES: Yeah. He told me in the course of the evening that his daughter, Dr. Eleanor Soltau, was in need of somebody to provide furlough relief. Of course, I knew my life was all arranged around that point; no way could I go to the mission field. But I was wrong!

BOB: God did butt in, right?

WES: Yeah. I laugh when I think how really true that is. You know, Dr. Pierce, it was only a matter of a few months after I contacted the mission that I was able to settle my affairs in the States and come here. In fact, I got out of the Navy on August 1 and by October 4 was here in Jordan; and I'm thoroughly enjoying it.

BOB: How long ago was that?

WES: A year—fourteen months really.

BOB: I'm thinking about all the adjustments, Wes. It's not like going to—say, Japan, where they're as sophisticated as we are. But here! These Bedouins are living as they did three or four thousand years ago. They don't even want what we have in the West; they don't even miss television and such; they don't covet our way of life. Aileen was telling me you have some patients who come by *camel* all the way from Saudi Arabia and such places clean here to this Jordan hospital for TB treatments.

WES: That's true. But they're a proud people.

BOB: I've been told that. And that they believe their religion is so great because for one thing they are the only ones who ever conquered Christianity—'way back when Istanbul was Constantinople, the center of Christianity. So you have your work cut out to get through to them with the Good News.

WES: That's true. But what they don't have is all the trappings of Islam; they don't have their mosques and minarets. It's pretty hard to carry the physical evidences of your faith when you're a nomadic people like the Bedouins. One of my patients told me the other day that he hadn't prayed more than twenty times in his life—a far cry from the five-times-a-day ritual of the Mohammedans! This is bound to make him more receptive to the gospel.

BOB: What do you love about them now that you're here? What can make the heart love them enough that you're willing to stay and work among them knowing that you don't have a whole lot of converts to show for your time and a lot of the health progress is comparatively slow? What makes you feel like you love 'em enough to put your life here?

WES: Well, in the first place, I'm quite sure this is where the Lord wants me. That's the most important thing. The second thing, the human aspect of it, is that they're a very affectionate, demonstrative people. They can scream madly at you, but they're also extremely affectionate. If you do the slightest thing for them, they'll be kissing your hand and just verbally making a great fuss over you. Then the next time you see them, they may bring a goat or a chicken or some Arab pastries and just be beaming madly. I mean, this kind of thing is very endearing; they're a very lovable type of people. Because Dr. Soltau is away, I haven't had time—I'm very tied to the hospital—but I'd like for one or two of us to get out among the tribes. We've made many friends out there, and we'd also like to do a little survey of what affect our Christian witness has had.

BOB: That's great, Wes. Now I'm interested in what you hope to do here in the areas of your particular interest.

WES: Well, I'm really a medical engineer. My background is much more toward research. Some people think that's a very strange thing, but it turns out to be a lot more useful than a lot of other things. Our limitations basically now are technical limitations and not limitations of knowledge. I'm limited somewhat by the fact that I don't have advanced degrees in chest work, but our biggest limitations are technical. We don't have the same things that any American hospital would have.

BOB: For instance? What piece of equipment could I do something about getting for you?

WES: Well, we need things for blood workups, and an odometer for doing hearing examinations. Oh—there's a whole lot of things, some big and some not very big or expensive. The Lord will ultimately provide for us; there are things, which, if people are really interested, we'd be glad to tell 'em about. We hesitate to *ask* for anything.

BOB: You're not asking; I'm asking you.

WES: I know and I appreciate it.

BOB: What I want you to know, Wes, is that I represent a lot of God's humble saints. Some of them are nearing the end of their life, but they still need to feel they have a reason for living another day and praying another day; and they just can't pray without wanting to *give* also. Not many of them have a whole lot to give, but they'd like to feel that they are a little part of the big things you and others are doing out here. They can't build a hospital, but they can put a little something in to keep our Samaritan's Purse filled so that we can partially meet needs like those you've mentioned, without anyone trying to be God. I know that only God can meet our overall need, you know. But we all want to love Him enough that we give something too.

WES: What can I say? You're right. What do we need? Recently, a visitor said the hospital looks bare. Maybe, that's true. We do need some more metal folding chairs—or something so we don't have to move these few from place to place on clinic days. And we'll need more beds—the inexpensive kind like we find here; not expensive ones like we use at home. I could go on, but . . .

BOB: That's okay, Wes. We'll be standing with you from now on. God bless you.

As always, Dr. Bob kept his word. It wasn't long before Samaritan's Purse was frequently opened to provide needed items for Annoor Hospital in Mafraq, Jordan, to encourage the doctor there who chose missions over chemistry when God butted into his life.

Bob Pierce, War Correspondent

At the onset of the Korean War, all but seven of the one hundred forty-four missionaries were ousted by the military. One who could not be kicked out was a Catholic priest, Father Connors; he had flown to Washington and been given credentials as a foreign correspondent—a United Nations war correspondent for all the Catholic Press. Dr. Bob was never one to back away from officialdom and bureaucracy. The following is his account of how he became a war correspondent:

"I arrived on the last civilian plane into Korea, bumped into Father Connors and asked him what the little cross on his cap meant. He was wearing an officer's uniform with a shoulder patch that said United Nations war correspondent, but he had no other insignia.

"How'd you get that?" I asked.

"He told me and gave me the names of who I should see in Washington. It took me two weeks to finish up what I had come to Korea to do; then I went straight to Washington. When I saw they weren't about to give me any correspondent's credentials, I said, 'Fine. But wait till you get a whiff of the stink that is

going to rise from your refusing me. I do a weekly broadcast on
ABC; I'm *qualified*. You gave credentials to the *Catholics*, but
denied accreditation to the *Protestants!*'

"Before the afternoon was over, they gave it to me; and I
flew right back, accredited as a U.N. war correspondent and
stayed with Father Connors. The two of us were there for the
whole war period. During that time I was doing broadcasts
from Korea about the plight of the Christians: widows, orphans, the G.I. babies that were being left on the dump
heaps—stories to try to shake people up. That was also when I
was able to shoot film footage for the first documentary of
Korea.

"A year later, the missionary film we shot in Korea began to
create a concern for the Christians there. Up till then, what did
anybody in our churches know about Korea? *Nothing*. They
were not aware that there was a powerful—not dominant—but
very sturdy Korean Christian Church that suffered persecution
as few churches have ever been called upon to suffer.

"It was the combination of our broadcasts, films, and the
stories I could tell from firsthand experience that opened doors
such as Princeton to me, to make a plea for Korea.

"Without the status of United Nations war correspondent,
none of this would have been available to me to share with the
world."

When I think of how Dr. Bob pulled off getting those credentials, it seems to me just about like what Paul did one time.
He asserted his rights as a Roman citizen in order that he would
not be prevented from preaching the gospel. It was never for
himself—for self-aggrandizement—that Bob Pierce did these
kinds of things; it was out of deep conviction of what God
wanted him to do at the time.

The Afghanistan Lamb

There's nothing like being in Eastern countries for bringing
to life the stories Jesus told. Here Dr. Bob and Dr. Christy
Wilson of Afghanistan talk over the story of the lambs. It was

1961 and there was still a Protestant church in Kabul, the capital of Afghanistan.

BOB: Christy, you've just let me listen on your little tape recorder to an Afghan shepherd calling his sheep. Now how did you get that, and why was it of interest to you particularly? A sheep's a sheep, after all.

CHRISTY: Afghan sheep are not your ordinary flock, Bob. Their skin is prized, for they're a special breed; the fur is expensive because it's taken from newborn lambs. The skin is small; therefore, it can take thirty to forty to make a lady's coat. It's called *karakul.*

BOB: Well, I know it's beautiful, but what a shame that it costs the lives of little lambs, especially when we think of the Twenty-third Psalm and of the wonderful pictures the Bible paints of God feeding and leading and carrying the little lambs close to His bosom.

CHRISTY: I know. I've often thought that myself. In fact, it was because of the story Jesus told that I went in search of a lamb and was able to record the shepherd calling his flock.

One of my teachers for the little Sunday School that meets in our home asked me if I could possibly get a little lamb so that she could have it to illustrate the lesson. So I started off, and 'way up in the mountains I located a shepherd who had a little lamb in his arms. He had a large flock, and that lamb had just been born that very day. It was pure white, and I thought, *What a wonderful illustration of Isaiah 1:18: ". . .* though your sins be as scarlet, they shall be as white as snow; though they be red like crimson, they shall be as wool" (KJV). That's the kind of wool the prophet was speaking about.

BOB: So did you buy this little lamb, Christy?

CHRISTY: When I asked the shepherd, he said, "You can't buy the lamb without its mother," so we started bargaining as to the cost. And, in the meantime, his main flock had wandered off some three hundred yards. That's when he made these strange sounds I recorded. Of course, I didn't keep my recorder at the ready so I had to ask him if he'd call his sheep again so I could get the sound on my tape. He demurred at that. And he explained, "If I call them again, they'll all crowd around because they were already close from hearing my first call."

It just made the Bible live for me, Bob; in this country we constantly observe things that look as if they are taken right out of the New Testament. These sheep *did* know that shepherd's voice—the special sound he made when calling them to him. I said to him, "What if someone else makes those strange sounds, will your sheep come?" He laughed and answered, "Oh, *no*. They won't follow anyone else; only me." I could tell he was speaking the truth, for there were other shepherds and sheep around; none of the other sheep made a move when he called.

BOB: Do the other shepherds use similar sounds?

CHRISTY: Yes, the sounds are similar, yet the sheep know the particular shepherd's *voice*—and they won't respond or follow another shepherd. They'll only go to their own shepherd.

BOB: Then the tenth chapter of John is really, *literally* true. Do you suppose that the occasion for Jesus using the lamb illustration was that there were sheep and lambs around at that time?

CHRISTY: I wouldn't doubt it for a minute. For instance, when John the Baptist proclaimed, "Behold the Lamb of God," it was near Passover season, and at that time the shepherds would be driving their lambs across the fords of Jordan to be sold for a sacrifice. The "Lamb of God who taketh away the sin of the world" was right in their midst!

BOB: If I remember rightly, don't the Muslims still sacrifice lambs as they did in the Temple days?

CHRISTY: That's right. They do—at the main feast, which commemorates the sacrifice of Isaac by his father Abraham. That's one reason there are so many sheep in the mountains around Kabul.

BOB: Did your Sunday School teacher get any more points out of this lesson?

CHRISTY: She certainly did. I took that little lamb, and she held it and the children were just thrilled to see a real, live, little white lamb and to hear the story of Jesus Christ, who is the Good Shepherd who gave His life for the sheep. They really listened as she told them all about how the sheep hear their own shepherd's voice and a stranger they will not follow. I believe none of those children will ever forget what they learned so graphically that day about the Lamb of God who takes away sin—their sin—as they hear His voice and confess their sin and follow Him.

Dr. Christy Wilson's beloved country, Afghanistan, is embroiled in a bitter civil war in which the Soviet Union is backing the Communist faction. Dr. Wilson is now a professor at Gordon Conwell Theological Seminary.

It's Too Far and Too Cold

Korea is famous for its early-morning prayer meetings. Dr. Bob shared with me his experience of a very special one.

"It was the week leading up to Easter, shortly after the end of World War II. The churches had just begun to get hold of their work again; the Bible Institutes were beginning to function after having been closed by the Japanese. I'd just had the privilege of preaching for the General Assembly of the Presbyterian Church and the General Conference of the Methodist Church. Now I was in the great port city of Pusan, where they have snow on the mountains all year round and it can be very cold in the morning at Easter time. Nevertheless, the Christian leaders were planning an outdoor sunrise service. They pointed out a hill that dominated the city and said, 'That's where we would like to hold our Easter service.'

"But," I said in amazement, "the people will have to walk. You're talking about a 5:00 A.M. service. This means that many will have to walk *two hours or more;* that will mean starting out at three o'clock in the morning and they'll freeze! Do you think anyone will come?"

"The pastors said quietly, 'They will come.'

"The meeting was scheduled, and I rode in a jeep as far as

the road went, then walked with some others toward the top of the hill. I was astounded. Just couldn't believe my eyes! Thousands of worshipers had gathered there on that mountain top in the bitter cold of that early morning. It was unforgettable, one of the most moving, heart-stirring services I ever was privileged to participate in. I'll never forget nor do I think I'll hear anything again like that singing of, 'Up from the grave He arose . . . Hallelujah, Christ arose!'

"I noticed tears running down the cheeks of many. I spoke just briefly, and, when the meeting was over, I turned to one of the pastors and said, 'I'll never know how you got this great host of people to walk all the way up this mountain at such an outrageous hour in such bitter cold.'

"The pastor explained, 'Look around; you'll see this is a plateau that can be seen by the whole city. This isn't the first time we've made this walk. Many of us have been forced to march up here with a bayonet in our backs. Even the Christians were made to bow at the Shinto Shrine: that shrine is the symbol not only of the *Japanese emperor*, but of his *deity*. Those whose Christian conscience would not let them submit, suffered unmercifully at the hands of the Japanese. Many were imprisoned; two hundred fifty pastors in Korea lost their lives rather than bow to the shrine of the emperor. They required this of us as a mark of patriotism.

" 'That's the reason so many were willing to walk these early hours and make the journey up this mountain. Because we're now free, we want to let the world know we worship *Jesus Christ*, the King of Kings and Lord of Lords. Oh, the joy of kneeling here this morning and giving our true worship to the One whom we truly love!'

"So, Franklin," Dr. Bob said, "as we commemorate the resurrection of our Lord, please remember that in some parts of the world Christians will have to worship in private, in secret—their lives at stake for loving Jesus Christ.

"If you find the headlines depressing and you're tempted to doubt whether or not the blessed gospel will survive the present onslought of atheism, communism, humanism, and materialism, let me tell you: 'One day yet, in God's own time, *all men everywhere* will bow and every tongue shall confess that Jesus Christ is King of Kings and Lord of Lords.'"

Pierce-Paksa

Dr. Bob's brief term as a psychological war expert had a surprise beginning and a heart-warming piece of encouragement. Here, he relates it:

"I was walking through the lobby of the Chosun Hotel on my way to the basement, for in those days only VIPs were given a room; I was just a foreign correspondent.

"'Pierce-Paksa! What are you doing here?' I turned quickly to see who was greeting me in the Korean term of respect for a pastor. I thought I was hearing things. But there stood a lovely Korean girl.

"'Pierce-Paksa!' she exclaimed again; she was almost in shock, for as an evangelist, to her I was a pastor. And by then all the Americans—missionaries and tourists—were gone. And here I was.

"'Well,' I answered, 'I am sleeping in the basement of this hotel and eating down there, too.'

"She looked horrified, for in her respect for me, she visualized me standing up on a platform preaching to about eighteen thousand people, so she asked, 'Why aren't you staying *up*stairs?'

"'There is no place, daughter,' I said, 'You know that only the high military are in this hotel now. Who let you in?'

"'I have a special reason that I will tell you in a minute. But first, Pierce-Paksa, I can get you a room.'

"'What do you mean?' I asked, and she astounded me by saying,

"'The psychological warfare specialists are all here. You are going to get a nice room—one of the best; you will have to share it with another man—'

"'Well, honey,' I chipped in, 'I don't want to pretend I'm

something I am not; I'd rather stay in the basement than do that.'

"But this girl knew what she was about; she was university trained.

" 'If you are preaching the gospel and telling people how they can find Jesus Christ and have their lives changed—if that isn't psychological warfare, then I don't have any brains at all. As far as I am concerned, you are an expert. You and I know that it is *God's* warfare, but nobody's going to ask me. So you are here as a specialist and eligible for a room.' She handed me a paper, had me sign it and register, and the rest of my two weeks there I had one of the best suites (with a fine man, though he was not a believer).

"Why did she do all this? She told me.

" 'Pierce-Paksa, this is why I had to get you out of that basement and find you a nice place to stay. It will please my mother. You don't *know* what it will mean to my mother!'

"She said, 'You know that when the Communists came in the first time, they walked through the halls of Severance Hospital and shot everybody—all the patients, all the doctors, all the nurses. They were all murdered. My older brother, who was the pride of my mother's heart and all our family, was about to become a doctor—he was studying at Severance University—and was one of those murdered in the hospital. But the comfort of my mother's heart is that, while you were preaching here in Seoul, my brother was one of those who walked one night out of the crowd and came forward and gave his heart to Jesus in answer to her lifelong prayers that he become a Christian. Her comfort now is that she knows he is in heaven waiting for us. She mentions it every day and thanks God that Pierce-Paksa came and that her son went to hear him and gave his life to Jesus those nine weeks before this horrible thing happened. We haven't lost him; we are going to see him again in heaven. When I go home and tell Mamma that I got you a room today, you don't know what it will mean to her and what it means to me.'

"It was like a little bit of heaven meeting that girl. That was *God* at work again!"

They Saved My Face

Dr. Bob was always keenly aware of the strategic part his interpreter played in his ministry in foreign countries. And he was quick to pay fitting tribute to these Christian nationals never forgetting that without them he was literally useless as preacher or evangelist. I like his tale of his first venture with an interpreter. He was in Shanghai, and his interpreter was Rev. Andrew Gih.

"I'd been trying to illustrate the difference between a born-again believer and someone who is not saved. 'Once you are saved, that doesn't mean you will never sin; but it means that you now have a new nature. Before, you loved sin; now, you hate it. Oh, you may fall into sin, but you'll want to get out of it as fast as you can.' I then used the analogy of a sheep and a pig. "Now you take a sheep: if it falls into a puddle and gets covered with mud, it can't get out of there fast enough because it has a *sheep nature*. It wants to be clean. But the minute a pig finds a puddle, he rolls in it, over and over, and there's hardly any way you can get him out of it because his *pig nature loves that mud puddle*. That's the difference between a Christian and a non-Christian; non-Christians are pigs."

"That's when Andrew exploded.

"He turned to me and said, *'You can't say that!* That's the filthiest name you can call a Chinese. You can call him an illegitimate son of an illegitimate mother—but you cannot use the word *pig*, or *swine*. That illustration cannot be used in China! It insults every living Chinese.'

"Of course he said all that to me in English. And I remember that the China Inland Missionaries in the audience were just rolling with laughter. The Chinese who were literate and educated and understood English were also laughing, but from a different point of view. They were seeing this smart aleck American getting his comeuppance in front of eighteen thousand people in the biggest city in China!

"After that experience, I suggested to Andrew that we compromise: 'Whenever I say something or use an illustration that doesn't fit China, you say what fits China. Just use my text and go from there.' So, that's exactly what he did, and we saw hundreds of people saved. According to some missionaries, there were over seven hundred and sixty people saved in those meetings. From then on, I'd speak thirteen seconds, Andrew would speak thirteen seconds, I'd speak twelve seconds and Andrew would speak twelve seconds, and 99 percent of the people thought Andrew was interpreting.

"Andrew took his outline and entirely departed from mine and preached his own sermon! I'd tell a joke and he would tell a joke, and the audience would just roar. I thought I was the biggest success since Milton Berle, but it turned out Andrew didn't tell the same joke that I did at all, because our American jokes often don't translate into Chinese. Most Chinese jokes are a play on words and even between one dialect and another, a joke is not translatable because if you can't make the play on the word, it's no joke.

"That's how Andrew and I preached together for three months. I doubt if he ever used three of my sermon outlines. He'd take any text I could think up, and he had a good sermon to preach and that's why I'm famous in China as a good preacher.

"The same is true of other interpreters, in other countries.

"Dear Dr. Hahn would take my raw sermons in Korea and polish them just as Andrew Gih had done in China. If I didn't put it in translatable Korean, he took the thought and rephrased it. So I have a reputation as a great preacher in Korea from one end to the other because the Koreans who didn't speak English—and almost none of them did in those days— have nothing but the memory of this beautiful prose of Dr. Hahn who took my simple things and put them into polished phraseology. He was a frail little man. He couldn't have weighed more than a hundred pounds or so, and in those days I weighed two hundred and ten pounds. When I'd get to giving my invitation, and start pleading with those people to turn to Christ and forsake their sins, oftentimes it would last twenty minutes, and he would match me—*decibel* by decibel—with all the urgency of Judgment Day right around the corner, as we pleaded with people to come to Christ.

"So, I say, God bless the faithful interpreters who, because they have cared enough to learn English, make it possible for people like me to do my part to carry out Christ's great commission."

Christlike Compassion

Compassion takes many forms, and Dr. Bob never missed an opportunity to show the love of Christ in the most practical way possible in the situation.

In 1977, he returned to Kalimantan to visit a man whom we had both met two years earlier, Bob Williams, better known as "Borneo Bob." With Hubert Mitchell, he had founded the "Go Ye Fellowship." Borneo Bob lived on the Kapuas River and had a wonderful little mission station there. Over the years, hundreds and hundreds of churches had been started by the faithful laboring of this special servant of God.

Kalimantan is now a part of Indonesia; but, right after World War II, it was known as Dutch Borneo and the Dutch government was responsible for administering this part of the world. The people along the river were riddled with disease and came to Bob Williams day after day pleading that he would do something for them. Not being a doctor, he could do very little except change bandages and administer aspirins. Finally, he pleaded with the Dutch government to send a doctor into the area. The Dutch informed him that they could not send anyone; however, they would be willing to have him come downriver to the capital, Potianak, and would give him a six-month course in basic medicine. Out of desperation, Borneo Bob did this and then returned to the jungle with a limited knowledge on how to treat certain fevers, etc. He still runs this clinic today and, when he comes up with something too complicated for him to handle, he calls by radio to Bethesda Baptist Hospital some two hundred miles away to get their advice.

Dr. Bob loved this man and his little spot on the river. Shortly before Dr. Bob's death, he went to Kalimantan to say good-bye to Borneo Bob and to see if there was something God wanted him to do. While he was there, on his way down to the river, he noticed a girl lying on a bamboo mat and asked Bob Williams what she was doing there. Bob Williams explained that she was dying of a form of cancer and had very few days to live. Dr. Bob's anger flared. "How come this girl is lying down there in the mud when she could be up there in that nice, clean clinic?" he stormed.

Borneo Bob explained that this girl was a jungle girl and preferred to be near the river where it was cooler, that she had specifically asked to be placed there for the day. Bob Pierce's heart broke. He went over to the girl, knelt down beside her, held her hand, and, rubbing her forehead, he prayed for her. After he prayed, she looked up and said something to him. He turned to Borneo Bob, who translated what she had said, explaining that with her disease and the unbearable pain she was unable to sleep and was saying, "If I could only sleep again, if I could only *sleep* again!" Bob Pierce began to cry, for he himself was dying of leukemia and had less than a year to live, and he knew what it was to be unable to sleep. He reached into his pocket and grabbed his bottle of sleeping pills. He gave it to Bob Williams and said, "You make sure she gets a good night's sleep from now on." Dr. Bob knew that he would have to go another ten days before he could get to Singapore and replace his medication—he knew that he would have to forfeit ten nights of sleep for this little girl.

By the time Dr. Bob arrived at his home in California, there was a letter waiting for him from Bob Williams stating that this girl had died and that one of the last things she had said was, "Please thank that kind man who gave me this medicine so that I could sleep."

Lausanne—A Foretaste of Heaven

In July 1974 thousands congregated in Lausanne for the Congress on Evangelism. The theme of the Congress was "Let the Earth Hear His Voice!"

The incredibly colorful scene in the great hall can best be described by that paean of praise in the Revelation:

Thou art worthy . . . for thou wast slain, and hast redeemed us to God by thy blood out of every kindred, and tongue, and people, and nation (5:9, KJV).

Of all the people present, no one was more at home than Dr. Bob. Joyously he mingled with God's people in their national garb; he was not a stranger to these Christians who were leaders of their countries. They had come from the heat of India's plains and the snows of Afghanistan, from Mongolia and Manila, from Japan and Jordan, from Norway and New Guinea. Bangladesh, Hong Kong, Vietnam, Brazil, Jakarta, China, Singapore, Malaysia, Nepal, the African republics, Korea—the list could go on and on.

There was scarcely an area represented in which Bob Pierce had not personally encouraged missionaries and Christian nationals, meeting needs as he found them unmet—sending funds in response to crisis situations (the stated *purpose* of Samaritan's Purse).

As delegates listened and learned and prayed and sang together and as fellowship blossomed and new friendships were made, the true purpose—reaching the world's yet unreached millions for Christ—could not be forgotten. A graphic reminder of this growing responsibility was the prominently displayed population clock which ticked on relentlessly—each tick marking an increase in the number of people who populate the earth.

For Bob Pierce, as for a host of others, "Lausanne '74" was a foretaste of heaven, with all the blessed reunions. And to the day he laid down his tools and checked in with the Lord of the

Harvest, the driving force in his life was to win others who would one day with him sing the song of the redeemed around the Great Throne.

11. Give, Give, Give

DR. BOB ONCE TOLD of a wealthy and influential businessman who responded to an appeal from his church with the angry comment, "As far as I can see, this Christian business is just one continuous give, give, *give.*"

"Which just goes to prove," said the astute Bob Pierce, "that a man can accidentally hit upon a great truth, even though he expresses it in a grouchy spirit."

The pastor who received that reply sat down and wrote to the man saying, "I want to thank you for the *best definition* of the Christian life I've ever heard. As near as I can see, you are correct: this 'Christian business,' as you call it, *is* indeed just one continuous give, give, give."

"That pastor is right on two scores," Dr. Bob said. "First, the very fundamentals of the Christian life begin with God giving what He didn't need to give, what He did not owe anybody, what—in the face of the disobedience and the arrogance and pride and egotism of man—He had every reason not to give. Yet, '*God so loved the world, that he gave his only begotten Son, that whosoever believeth in him should not perish, but have everlasting life*' (John 3:16, KJV).

"God gave His son Jesus Christ; Jesus Christ gave His life a ransom for many. The great, loving heart of God surrounds us so that we can only say, 'Surely goodness and mercy has followed me all the days of my life.' In the light of all this giving to us, what should be our response?

"*Second*," Dr. Bob continued, "and the part the grouchy man didn't like—is that the Christian life from man to God is likewise giving. Not that we really have anything to give God. What could you give that God doesn't already have? Are you going to give Him a compliment? He has millions of angels to warm His heart whose worship and compliments are of far greater purity, holiness, and worthiness than yours or mine! What is it that you're giving to God that you're so proud about?

"Of course you don't have to give. God isn't going to twist your arm to make you dig into your pockets or reach for your checkbook.

"Actually it is a *privilege* to give to God's work. I feel so sorry for the Christian who responds to an appeal to help some missionary cause with the gripe, 'You're always asking for money.'"

Sometimes Dr. Bob would answer this kind of thinking by telling them something a father shared with him one time:

I had a little boy, our first child, and oh, what a joy he was to his mother and me. But there's no disputing that he was always costing me something. Everyday he needed food and milk; there were clothes and shoes to buy—and he liked to get a new toy. There were all kinds of things he needed and wanted, and it all took money. Then, when he was just four years old—he died! And that little boy has not cost me a cent ever since.

Dr. Bob would let that story make its impact, then go on to emphasize that Christ's business is a live concern. It doesn't run without money.

We all know that a need is an unfailing sign of life. A ministry that constantly has current needs is alive and going somewhere. Anything that's dead won't trouble people with appeals; won't give them any opportunities to do something worthwhile by giving to God.

What about tithing?

Dr. Bob was always quick to state his position on scriptural tithing. He'd say: "I believe in tithing. In Deuteronomy we find God speaking to His children about tithing." And he would ask, "Do you tithe? And does any part of your tithe go specifically for orphans and widows? In the law and command-ment of God it's not only a matter of *how much* you give, but also *what you give it for,* that makes your Christian giving really tithing. The tithe is to go to the Levite—that's the pas-tor, the Christian Education Director, the other ministerial helpers who work full time, and yes, even the janitor of the church. But that's just part of it. The Bible likewise tells us that the tithe is to go to the stranger and the fatherless and the widows, because God cares about these people.

"Tithing is fine *as a baseline* for giving. We go on from there if we're growing in the Lord and thankful for His goodness to us. We don't reckon percentagewise as our heart is broken with the things that break the heart of God. And we give without the extra motivation of a tax write-off! One of these days—and I think it may not be far off—governments, and in particular the U.S. government, are going to rescind the tax exemption for giving to churches or to charity. We won't be able to count on a big deduction for giving. When that day comes, some of the Christian programs that are presently haul-ing in millions of dollars are going to fold up. Those of us who never did rely on such exemption are not going to fold up because we have relied instead on the Lord's promise, 'My God shall supply all your need according to his riches in glory by Christ Jesus' (Phil. 4:19, kjv). The saints who love Jesus are going to give just as much when they get no tax deduction for it as when they did. I'd stake my ministry on that!

"Make room in your heart for the helpless, hopeless, and homeless widowed and orphaned. Stand by the work of your missionaries and the work of those faith mission groups, the faithful ones who preach Christ and hold forth the message of the gospel through the blessed Word of God. Remember them in your prayers. Stand by them; it is the command of God, it is the demand of God. And it will involve *giving.*

"In Jesus Christ we find revealed the concern of God for strangers, for widows, for orphans, for those who have nothing.

It is the concern and the responsibility of the follower of Jesus Christ to do something about these needs. *Wherever you find men and women who really love Jesus Christ,* you find the compassion of Christ spilling out of them to meet human need."

I remember something that Dr. Bob once said about suffering that spoke to me as a parent. He said, "One of the things that's wrong in America is that we hardly make our children feel that anything is worth suffering for; and the result is that they're bored with life. Perhaps one of the greatest gifts we can give our children is an excitement about what they can be involved in—something that will make a difference in their world. We need to imbue them with the fact that there are some things that are worth suffering and sacrificing for—that spiritual values are the greatest investment."

He would often challenge his audience with, "You can't take your money with you, but you can send it on ahead."

He was quick to remind people that God asks for other things besides money.

"There's something everybody can give Him. There are some things God asks for, things within your power to hold back.

"There's *love;* you can deny God love.

"There's *obedience;* the Bible says that God wants obedience and not sacrifice.

"There's *service;* God uses people who want to be used. He won't force you away from what you're doing, to the tasks He would like to have you do. If ever you are used in His service, it will be because one day you came and humbly presented your body a living sacrifice, willing to give your life for Him where He would have you go.

"Living begins for the Christian, with going a step beyond believing, to giving. The compensations in this life are the peace and joy, the radiance of being in His will.

"I'm reminding you that maybe the thing your church needs the most is for you to give a little time: time enough to put you in the prayer meeting on Wednesday night; time enough to be there not only so the pastor is encouraged by your presence in the pew, but so that neighbors around you see the influence of your presence in church.

"Yes, to be a Christian *is* to give, give, give: but not just money."

It needs to be said that Bob Pierce didn't preach one thing and practice another. He never asked anyone to give more than he, himself, was willing to give. Often, he emptied his own pocket, simply trusting God to meet his needs, even as he asked his supporters to do. He did give his time, his talents, his whole self to God—and that included giving money.

Dr. Bob on Memorials

Another form of giving about which Dr. Bob was outspoken was *memorials*. I've heard him give his views on that subject:

"There's a little cemetery on the south side of Los Angeles," he would begin, "where my father and mother are buried and over their graves is a little marble marker. On it is just their name, the day they were born and the day they died. It wasn't put there to be a reminder to all passersby that my father and my mother once lived and walked on this earth. No. It's there just so that we who loved them can find their earthly resting place.

"But in that cemetery are many costly tombstones and mausoleums. These were erected, I'm sure, by loving hearts who were so broken by the loss of that loved one, that they felt they had to make some enduring mark upon their community, something that would make some claim upon the attention of future generations that their loved one had lived and walked there. But time goes by. After a while no one even remembers who is buried there; nobody visits that cemetery anymore; the city takes over the land, and what was intended as a permanent memorial is wiped from the face of the earth."

While he had these strong convictions, Dr. Bob was balanced in his thinking about this and most other things. He would go on to say,

"Really, there can be no adequate memorial to you and your life except *what you are*—not just the things you leave behind—it's what *you were* while you walked on Earth."

Then, as always Dr. Bob's mind turned to his beloved missionaries.

"I love to work for missionaries," he would say with his face glowing, "because so often I find enduring memorials that are not built of stone or marble. They are the memorials that live on and on in the lives of students whom they trained who then trained other students—men and women who, by what they were and did while they were here on earth, made some difference in some part of the world in the name of Jesus Christ. A difference that forever goes on because those who were in darkness now are in light, and the light goes on and on and on—those who were in hopeless ignorance have been made literate, and the fruit of their literacy lives on.

"Oh, there are enduring memorials to be built. What kind are you building?" he would ask. . . . "Enough money to buy expensive things to leave behind when you die, hoping that those you leave them to will identify with you? Better, my friend, that you should leave an enduring example.

"I realize that there are significant memorial buildings. I've walked in the mission fields and seen a hospital that someone built instead of a mausoleum, and I've admired their wisdom. I've seen a score of such hospitals where some name is identified with surcease from pain, relief from suffering. I've been in schools built with the legacy of a lifetime of hard work by someone who loved the Lord and left every cent they'd saved to missions, so that a school could be built. And for generations after, little children were taught not only to read the Bible, but to understand what is going on in the world around them.

"Yes, these kinds of enduring memorials need to be built. The vast majority that have really blessed the world were built by Christian men and women with serious intent. Their purpose was to see that what they had accumulated during their lifetime was left specifically to glorify God and really minister to men and women, boys and girls for whom Christ died."

Then, Bob Pierce the *soul-winner* would come to the fore as he concluded his memorial dissertation with the question, "What kind of a memorial will you leave behind? A good thing to think about *today!* What are you leaving that will endure after you've gone?

"Have you done anything for Jesus and the lost that will keep on bearing fruit?

"Have you led a soul to Christ, someone who, after you've passed into the presence of the Lord, will still be ministering in the harvest fields, and leading others who, after they themselves have gone on, will still be leading others to Christ? Now *there's* a memorial that will endure!"

The 'Little' Givers

In the same warm, loving way in which he spoke of the "little" people—needy, neglected, forgotten people—Dr. Bob often spoke of the "little" givers. And he described them as the people *who care about Jesus,* who want to *lay up treasure in heaven,* whose chief aim is not to get rich, but just to please God. "And that is, as near as I understand the Word of God, about the biggest thing anybody can do," he would say.

There was one man, in particular, that Dr. Bob used as an example, a Michigan farmer named Lee. I'll let you read Dr. Bob's own words about this "little" giver.

"Except for large gifts from foundations, the gifts that are given to Samaritan's Purse are from supporters who give as the widow gave her mites. In *God's* sight, their gifts are *large.*

"One man who gave consistently, intrigued me for some reason. He was *so* faithful. One year he gave the entire amount he got for his bean crop—about six hundred dollars. He gave recklessly to Jesus, and I would write him and encourage him, telling him what his gifts were doing. When I had to go to Detroit one time, I said to myself, *Michigan is Michigan; wherever my friend Lee lives, I'm gonna go and see him and thank him personally.* I rented a car and learned it was one hundred and twenty-five miles to the little town where he lived.

Finding him was something else: twenty to thirty miles along a barely paved road, then a dirt road. Finally I found his farm-house with its ancient barn.

"The sun was just going down. I saw a stooped figure of a man as I pulled into this farmyard. Obviously, he would have been six feet, if he hadn't been bent with fatigue and weari-ness—a man in his late seventies. He walked toward me and I said, "Lee, by any chance? My name is Bob Pierce."

"He just stood there for a moment then said, 'Dr. *Bob!* What are *you* doing 'way out here?'

"I answered, 'God sent me here, Lee, to see you—and any-way I wanted to find out what kind of a man you are, and to get to know you.'

"Well, he took me inside a house that his parents had home-steaded more than a century ago. We walked in the backdoor to a kitchen with an old-fashioned wood stove, not a modern cooking range. He had an old mangy dog that was his only companion. We sat and talked, and he told me that he and his wife had once, many years before, driven three hundred miles to hear me speak. They gave to our work then, and continued to give regularly through the years as they heard me on the radio.

"Lee lives his life in that kitchen, when he's not out breaking his back farming. He said the house was so lonely for him without his wife that he had closed it all up except the kitchen.

"He told me, 'I've outlived all my friends. I go to a little church in town, and they call sometimes to see if I've died in the night or something.' Then he said, 'Dr. Bob, the only joy I have is to send what money I can to you—to *Samaritan's Purse* — for all those needs. I don't need anything.'

"I thought, *I doubt if he even has one suit; and here he is saying he doesn't need anything.* I looked around that kitchen. There was nothing that had any value except, perhaps, the radio that brought him his gospel programs.

"The Bible says there's a day coming when the last shall be first—the least shall be the greatest. And that is when these little hidden-away givers that nobody ever writes books about or asks them to make public appearances on TV, will come into their own. *Jesus* will parade them. (My friend Lee's wife will be right alongside him there.) Jesus will show them off along with that widow who gave her all; and in sight and sound of all the rest of us who may sometimes crow over how much we've done for Jesus, He will draw them to Himself and say, 'Well done, thou good and faithful servant . . . enter thou into the joy of your Lord.'

PART FOUR

Dr. Bob, Remembered

12. You Call *That* Missions!

IT WAS NOT JUST for the suffering "little" people, that Bob Pierce's heart bled. It was also for the missionaries.

Jeanette Lockerbie heard this story from one of the Bangladesh missionaries who lived through the bloody War of Liberation (where her own daughter nursed the wounded freedom-fighters and sheltered young girls from the enemy soldiers). Jeanette and missionaries, Dr. Phil Parshall and his wife Julie, met aboard the *Logos* ship in '81. And when Bob Pierce's name was mentioned, Phil and Julie glowed.

"I'll never forget one thing about Bob Pierce. It was in 1972," Phil said. "The barbarous war that had brought Bangladesh (nation of the *Bengalees*) to birth, had ended in victory for them—but oh, the cost! Not only to the nationals, but to the missionaries who had stayed through it all. We were wiped out, physically and emotionally; we were at the end of our endurance.

"Then Bob Pierce showed up in the capital, Dacca, looking, as always, for ways to be God's Samaritan. He rounded up every last one of us missionaries in Dacca and invited us all to the Intercontinental Hotel (at that time the country's finest and a place that none of us could afford to go).

"Bob took us all to a nice big room and just sat down with us and *listened*. He let us pour out all the pent-up feelings, the agony, the horror—everything we needed to drain off. He didn't question; he didn't lecture; he didn't give us advice. He just 'sat where we sat'; he was *there for us*. He related to us in our total weariness.

"When we had pretty well unloaded and we felt relieved, he shared with us some of his own trauma and trials in carrying out what God had given him to do.

"Then he treated us all to a great meal.

"Who but a man of deep understanding and supreme compassion would have thought to do such a thing for all of us, to consider that meeting some *missionaries'* traumatic needs and ministering to us as he did, was 'missionary work.'

"I can say for all of us that we left Bob Pierce that day, renewed in our spirit and more able to keep on going."

Donuts and Orange Juice

Jeanette was sitting across the desk from me in my office in Boone not long ago, and she said, "Would you like to hear something Bob Pierce did in Hong Kong while I was there one time?"

I nodded and she went ahead.

"Enroute to Indonesia I was staying with a Christian and Missionary Alliance missionary, Gladys Jasper, a dynamo like Bob, who was programming my writing seminars. At the time she was coordinating the plans for an all-Asia Christian Communications Seminar. The phone kept ringing with requests from men who badly needed to attend, but didn't have the money for plane fare. This was the first all-Asia conference of its kind and people were invited from Korea, Pakistan, Bangladesh, Indonesia—all the Asian countries. I heard Gladys promise to do what she could and get back to them. Then— Bob Pierce called and I heard Gladys lay the case before him. As she turned from the phone her face had relaxed. Samaritan's Purse would come through. And they did!

"Were you at that conference, Jeanette?" I asked.

"Oh yes," she said, "and that's another tale! Want to hear it?"

"Sure," I agreed, "who wouldn't?" and this is what she told me:

"Three weeks later I returned to Hong Kong, and again Bob phoned while I was with Gladys in h⌐ᵢ home. He was inquiring about the food and accommodations. Gladys informed him and his comment was, 'Morrison House (a Chinese Center) is okay. But we'd better do something about the *food* or you won't have the energy to go through a heavy week. Meet me for lunch, and I'll give you a check.' I could have been there, Franklin, for Bob had told Gladys to bring me along, but I had an appointment to speak to the Hong Kong Kiwanis Club that day. When I got back, Gladys showed me a check for five thousand dollars."

"What did that do?" I asked.

"Oh, *what did it do?* You would have had to be there to get that answer. For breakfast we had *real milk*—from a carton. We had Tropicana *orange juice*, both of which were 'way out of reach' for both nationals and missionaries who were present. That money provided, besides added nutrition in the regular meals, coffee and tea breaks with Danish pastries and even *donuts*. These were times of real fellowship and interaction with one another. I still remember how wonderful it was to sit with the brethren from Pakistan, Bangladesh, and India and see them enjoying being together—men whose countries, over the years, had been bitter enemies.

"And Bob was right. That food provided energy for the fourteen-hour days of study and deliberations. Out of that October '76 'Tell Asia' gathering emerged The Asian Christian Communications Fellowship (ACCF) for which I serve as a writing consultant. And whenever some of us get together in any of these countries, someone is sure to mention the orange juice and the donuts, that one-of-a-kind special treat made possible by a man of exceptional insight that didn't stop there."

"And," I remarked to Jeanette, "some folk would complain, 'You call *that* missions!'"

On another occasion, Dr. Bob wrote his supporters "after the fact":

> I've just done something you would want me to do. Knowing that Christmas is a time when the missionary children come home from boarding school and the families are together, I've left money for each family, to be used expressly so that the children will remember *one glorious unskimpy meal*—when the family can be a little reckless about buying food.

Dr. Bob tells of a friend in Hong Kong who was so tuned in to the Samaritan Purse ministry that he cashed a "faith check" for ten thousand dollars, confident that in response to God's voice His people would have sent in the money before the check could reach the bank in the States. In the *next few hours* the Lord sent one of the largest single gifts the Purse had ever received—*ten thousand dollars* to cover that check!

Everybody needs a miracle from time to time. And the Lord knew that Bob Pierce was always willing to be His vehicle to deliver a miracle. There was no end to the ways he found to let the Lord use him as he gave himself for people in countries that were in a perpetual state of crisis.

Tickets to Freedom and Service

In the domino-toppling days when refugees and missionary evacuees were streaming out of Laos, Cambodia, and Vietnam, Dr. Bob more than once used his airline credit cards—rather, he let a missionary use them. Some were fleeing to safety; others, to countries where arriving refugees desperately needed their help. Jeanette had been in and out of Hong Kong a lot during that time, and on one occasion she heard the story of a missionary from Vietnam who was posted by his mission to the Philippines to work among refugees.

It was mandatory that anyone entering the Philippines have either an ongoing or else a return ticket. He had neither; nor did he have the money to buy one. So the agent refused to board him and his wife. What to do? God wanted him in the

Philippines. The airline agent was impatiently urging him to leave the window. Then an arm reached over his shoulder and he heard a voice say, "Here, use my credit card, Buddy." It was Bob Pierce.

The following day Jeanette ran into Dr. Bob Pierce and told him what she'd just heard. Then she said, "Bob, what you did at the airport for those missionaries must have made God and all the angels happy." He grinned, then said very soberly, "Jeanette, there was no way I could *not* have been in that check-in line at that very time. It was no accident."

When It's Horses They Need

In one of Dr. Bob's Samaritan letters, he wrote the following concerning Afghanistan:

> While I was a twelve hours' drive, high in the mountains out of Kabul, I found two wonderful British nurses who serve as midwives and perform all kinds of emergency medical tasks. They desperately need horses to ride through the deep snow during winter months when roads are closed and the distances often too great for them to otherwise reach many women who are in the most acute pain and whose lives and those of their babies are in danger.
>
> With horses, however, each of these nurses could cross rivers, climb steep mountain trails, and press to desperate emergencies otherwise impossible to reach. Your gifts permitted the Samaritan's Purse to not only buy each nurse an excellent horse, but to buy saddles and pay for stabling and food to keep the horses through the bitter winter cold. God alone knows what places the love of Christ will reach during these days of fleeting opportunity because two nurses could get there in time by horseback. *HORSES:* you call *that* missions!

Mattresses, Plastic Sheets, Guitars

Dr. Bob's great joy on his missionary journeys was preaching the gospel. He had visited Lil Dickson's Mustard Seed Trade

School. This was for boys out in the bush and twenty-two of them committed themselves earnestly to Christ.

Of course he touched other places and he wrote of one trip,

In the city of Jakarta, I discovered a House of Death—a place hidden behind a school for the blind, where hopelessly doomed tubercular people are sent to await death. It's such a depressing experience to visit there that only a few very dedicated people do. Glen and June Garber visit there regularly.

One thing especially broke my heart. More than forty of these dear people with no one coming to see them, no more medical hope, no place in society, just waiting for death, were lying on beds with only springs—no mattresses! Of course, we immediately took Samaritan's Purse money to buy mattresses, but then discovered that the mattresses would be hopelessly ruined in a matter of days if they didn't have plastic sheets, as many of the people cannot control their bodily functions and there is an inadequate staff. The attitude seems to be, who wants to take care of the folks for whom there is no hope? But somehow, I couldn't help but feel that if Jesus were to visit Jakarta, it's quite possible that the very first place He'd head for would be this hidden place to visit these forsaken souls, even though they are Muslim or Hindu, and it's hard for Protestants to be able to do any open witnessing to them. Still, I believe Jesus would hasten lest *one* die without having known some compassionate touch from a loving Savior who died for them.

At the school for the blind in the front of this place, there were also desperate needs, especially for something to help these dear people *do something for themselves.* I found that several had musical talent and the most desired instrument for these people were guitars, so we left the money for four guitars to be purchased. When I go again, we'll see how well these guitars are used for comfort and ministry to these people handicapped in the midst of a religion that offers little compassion because everything is supposed to be just the "will of Allah." Again, while we couldn't choose the songs they might learn to play on their guitars, we could let them know from whose loving hand the guitars were given.

Doubtless, some people would seriously question, "Is *that* missions?"

Turkeys

Dr. Bob Pierce was always looking for ways to make missionaries lives a little easier and doing something a little special for them—something that nobody else would do and something that because of the cost they might not do for themselves.

One year he had the idea of supplying every missionary family in New Guinea with a turkey for Christmas. Now, of course, there are no turkeys in New Guinea and no missionary family had ever had a turkey dinner while in New Guinea. Some missionary families had been there over thirty years and had never seen a turkey. Bob was not going to let that be a stumbling block to him. He knew that if there was a will there would be a way. He started inquiring as to where in the world he could get some turkeys. He said, "I want to give every missionary family a turkey." The first answer was, there are no turkeys in New Guinea, but Bob kept on. Finally he learned that the only country in all of Southeast Asia that raised turkeys was the island of Australia. Now Australia is directly south of New Guinea and the only city where he could buy these was Sydney, approximately twenty-five hundred miles away. Instead of being discouraged by the distance, he worked out a deal with a friend of his in Australia to buy the turkeys, have them frozen and then to have Quantus Airlines fly them to Port Moresby, the capital city of Papua New Guinea. There a Missionary Aviation Fellowship plane made several round trips from Port Moresby to the interior of West Irian, New Guinea, where the turkeys were unloaded, put in huge freezers and kept frozen until these MAF pilots were able to distribute them one by one.

Samaritan's Purse received hundreds of thank you letters from missionary families all over that island, thanking Dr. Bob for making *that* Christmas extra special for them and their loved ones.

Some would say, "You'd call *that* missions!"

Sometimes Samaritan's Purse is opened—perhaps emptied—in response to an appeal from one of God's servants who has exhausted every other channel. Such a letter came from Ethiopia. The missionary wrote:

> This must be this year's most hopeless good cause! I have been trying to convince myself that it is so hopeless that there is no point in troubling anybody else with it when there are so many other well-publicized and worthy famines in the world, especially in Africa this year.
>
> What has finally compelled me to make some sort of effort, however unlikely, has been the little pile of humanity that has been sitting outside our back door for the last two weeks. They are the remains of a family from the Hammer tribe, the flotsam that gets washed up by the fierce pressures of tribal cultures that have had none of the influence of Christianity to temper the raw injustices of a totally pagan society. The family consists of a remarkably cheerful mother and five young children, probably under the age of eight. The husband died some years ago and, according to the inscrutable rules of Hammer society, the woman may not marry again, as she remains the personal property of the dead man's family because it was their cattle that bought her. If there is any brother or relative who cares to "take her on," she may go to him as a "spare" wife for as long as he cares to look after her, but when food is scarce these unfortunate widows and their children are thrown out to find some other man if they are lucky. It is these poor creatures who always suffer first in the lean months that come every year when the meager bit of grain is all gone and everyone is waiting for the next year's crop to ripen.

Bob didn't turn his back, shut his eyes, nor close his ears to their need. He emptied the Purse.

Still another appeal came from a missionary working in a reformatory for teenage girls in the Orient.

> Over five hundred of the six hundred and fifty girls are suffering from diseases caused by the filthy conditions. There's no soap with which to keep their bodies clean enough to avoid infectious dis-

eases, and no vitamins to help build up a resistence to scabies and other ills caused by malnutrition.

Another plea that came was for funds to buy food for foreigners—missionaries, some of them—who had been thrown into Asian jails. Having no local families to carry in food which is the customary thing, these men and women have to survive their sentence without outside help.

Dr. Bob's summation to his supporters was, "Oh, my beloved friends, let us take these heartbreaking needs to our heavenly Father who cares for even the sparrow that falls; who is waiting for us to share His love and the good news of His Son—that not one may be lost!"

What is "missions?"

Dr. Bob held this philosophy: "Whatever God tells us to do for someone who can't do it for himself, we *should* do. And since it is God who is telling us to do it—we *can* do it.

He would not have been one bit perturbed to hear anyone question, "You mean you call *that* missions!"

A Thousand Dollars for Underwear

"It was winter in Korea," Dr. Bob said, "On a snowy, 18-degree day a missionary took me to see something I've never forgotten. In an old icehouse abandoned by the Americans after the War, there were over two hundred men and women whom many people called beggars. Actually most of them were old and sick; some *may* have been beggars, but all of them were people who had nobody to care for them. There they lay on the dirt floor, some too sick to move. There was no heat; they huddled under rags and some filthy old blankets. At least fifty of the two hundred had no shoes and were barefoot in that cold. They had no food except the sacks of flour someone had given them; nothing to mix it with, no vegetables, no meat—nothing to make it one bit appetizing. It was like eating wallpaper paste; but it was all the food they'd had for days!

"What did we do? I'll tell you what we did. With the

missionary I went to the marketplace where we bought over a
thousand dollars worth of long, winter underwear, enough so
that everyone of those needy people would have something to
keep out the bitter cold. Then we bought three hundred dollars worth of stockings, and we left some money to buy shoes
for the little orphan children who were also among them.

"We didn't stop there, however. Though the people were so
poor and many too sick to do much for themselves, we wanted
to encourage them, to help them regain some self-respect. So
we bought a spaghetti-making machine. With some of the flour
they were given, they could make and sell some spaghetti and
with the money they could buy some fish.

"Then we bought them a rope-making machine and straw
fibre from which they make rope. Some of the men could thus
be enabled to help themselves.

"Underwear, stockings, shoes, a spaghetti-making machine,
a rope-making machine? Somebody says, 'Is *that* missions?'
Yes, that's missions. The missionary in this case was a Presbyterian elder (a man with no seminary education or degrees)
who had learned of the plight of these people. He had gotten
them together and poor though it was, had arranged this place
where they could stay. He had helped them with materials to
make straw shelters inside the walls of that old icehouse. He
solicited from the relief agencies flour and discarded blankets
that no one else wanted. He had been carrying on Bible studies
with them: sick and dirty as they were, they had their *prayer
meeting every morning.*

"We can sit in solemn conclaves and discuss what is and what
is not missionary work. Meanwhile, the missionaries are over-
worked and under-equipped and pressed on every side because they labor in the midst of needs that are never-ending.

If it's something that is breaking the heart of a compassionate
God, then—yes—you can call it missions.

Typesetter, Camera, Printing Press

In his Samaritan newsletter following his trip to the new
nation of Bangladesh, Dr. Bob wrote:

While I was in Dacca, a great group of young people from all over Europe and Asia arrived in the port city of Chittagong. They were with the training ship *MV Logos* that plies Asian ports. They clear the decks and hold a tremendous book fair for the public. Meanwhile these young people who give six months to two years in this ministry, form teams and go out all over the area witnessing and distributing Christian literature. It was one of the greatest opportunities I've ever known for getting the gospel to this Muslim country with its some ninety million souls.

Where did all this *Bengali* literature come from? The largest producer of *Bengali* Christian literature (the sixth largest language block in the world) is the Bible Literature Center in the city of Chittagong.

Some years had passed and Dr. Bob had gone on into the presence of our Lord and Savior, when an appeal came to us from the Director of this literature ministry. With an ever-increasing opportunity to spread the Word and almost nobody else producing *Bengali* material, the equipment was hopelessly inadequate. New typesetting, photographic, and printing machinery was costly but necessary if they were to move into the twentieth century and be able to compete with Communist literature that was readily available.

The need of *Literature for Bangladesh* would have burdened Bob Pierce's heart. As I prayerfully considered this request, I could almost hear him cheering us on with "That's a Samaritan's Purse-type need; send the check, Franklin." We did—for the full amount, $57,500. The cabled response of the delighted missionaries and their Bangalee colleagues said it all: "*We prayed* that our Hallelujahs would reach you!"

Wheelchairs and More Wheelchairs

Garth Hunt, president of *Living Bibles* of Canada and former Bob Pierce side-kick, tells of taking Dr. Bob through a hospital in Vietnam where the more than three thousand wounded, crowded two to a bed, were literally rotting. Many were amputees and because there was no way they could leave the hospital, conditions could only get worse. It was then that

Bob Pierce made a commitment to provide *forty wheelchairs a month* so that these amputees could go home. And one of the great things about Bob was that he *always kept his commitments.* Just six weeks after his visit in that hospital we went out to the airbase on the edge of Saigon to receive the first shipment of wheelchairs and medical supplies flown in from the West Coast of the States.

You would have thought it was Christmas the way we handled and fondled those wheelchairs! Now, by God's help, we were going to be able to put love into a tangible form; not just witnessing about it and preaching it to the wounded soldiers, but by actually demonstrating it in a practical way. Within an eight-year period, we distributed well over three thousand wheelchairs all over Vietnam. To quote Bob's adage, "We earned the right to be heard."

Bob's daughter Sharon, of all his children, shared most the compassion that God had given Bob. She would work in Vietnam right by her father's side. She'd walk through the hospital, see the amputees, and she, too, would break into tears; she looked for ways to encourage her father to do even more. She was not afraid to visit the dying, she was not afraid to be in a war. But she was afraid of seeing these needs and not doing anything about them.* She had said, "Daddy, you're not going to just *pray* for these men, you are going to *do* something." And Dr. Bob did something.

The wheelchair gifts were the beginning of one of the greatest ministries of social concern, evangelism, and Bible distribution that had ever been conducted in Vietnam, and it was carried on right until Vietnam fell. With each kit containing hygienic items, a Scripture portion provided by the Pocket Testament League was included. Doors swung wide open for us in training camps, rehabilitation centers, in camps for Viet-

---

*The Los Angeles Times, (January 31, 1967), in an article titled "Pain, But No Complaining" documented the contribution Dr. Bob Pierce's daughter Sharon was making in the amputee ward, and in other humanitarian projects in Vietnam.

Cong prisoners, and—interestingly enough—the doors of government opened to us. A new day dawned for the evangelical church in Vietnam! The Christians' *demonstrations* of love spoke louder than their words.

Apples and Seed Faith

In 1977, Dr. Bob Pierce and I were in Papua New Guinea which is an independent country which recently got its independence from Australia. In Papua New Guinea, you could buy Australian apples. Big beautiful red and yellow apples. On the other half of the island of New Guinea is West Irian. West Irian is formerly Dutch New Guinea which is now known as West Irian under the control of Indonesia. Restrictions there are very, very tight and they don't allow imported goods to come into the country. However, when Dr. Bob and I were in Papua New Guinea, we made plans to go to West Irian and Bob thought of something to take that would be unique and special. He thought of apples. He knew that the missionaries there, and especially the missionary children at the Alliance school in Sentani would probably never get an apple all year long. So he bought three cases of apples so each child could have three apples.

We landed at Sentani and spent the night with our dear Mission Aviation Fellowship pilots. The next morning, Bob was asked to address the student body. Bob had these cases of apples placed at the back of the little auditorium. He went up front with an apple in his hand and he spoke, taking the text of Matthew 13: 3–8:

And he spake many things unto them in parables, saying, Behold, a sower went forth to sow; And when he sowed, some seeds fell by the wayside, and the fowls came and devoured them up: Some fell upon stony places, where they had not much earth: and forthwith they sprung up, because they had no deepness of earth: And when the sun was up, they were scorched; and because they had no root, they withered away. And some fell among thorns; and the thorns sprung up, and choked them: But other fell into good ground, and brought forth fruit, some a hundredfold, some sixtyfold, some thirtyfold (KJV).

Bob then took this little apple, broke it open and took out a seed. He said, "This seed is like the Word of God, which is mentioned in this parable, and if you were to take this little seed and plant it out here in the ground and water it, someday it would spring up as a little plant; and if it continued to get water and sunlight, it would grow up to be a big tree. After a period of time, it would get to a point where the tree itself would bear fruit. This can be like you; if you take the Word of God and plant it in your heart, the Word of God will grow inside of you, and someday you will be able to produce fruit by leading others to Jesus Christ."

Bob went on to tell that simple story. Many children's hearts were touched that day with Bob's illustration of the apple. And then to illustrate it even further, he let every child take three apples home: two reds and one yellow. This was a tremendous treat for this school; for they had never had apples for their students before that day, and they've probably not had any since. But Bob Pierce cared enough not only to provide them a small treat, but he knew that he would illustrate it with the Scripture so that it would have an everlasting meaning. Some may say, you call that *missions?*

Where It All Began

The greatest missionary program ever planned and carried to its ultimate fulfillment was *God sending His Son into the world.*

The Lord Jesus, although He was and is "the Word," did not stop (or even start, in many instances) with preaching. He didn't set the multitude down and preach to them for an hour or two while they were hungry. He first fed them. When the leper came pleading, "Lord, if you will, you can make me whole," the Lord justified the man's faith in Him. Can you imagine what it meant to that leper to have someone *touch* him—a leper! That was enough to make Jesus "unclean." What did Christ do? He reached out and *touched* him. Nobody touches a *leper!* Jesus did. He didn't just preach, "Heal the sick, cleanse the leper"; He *did* it. The man was made whole— and there was no way he could keep quiet about it! He blazoned the Good News wherever he went, Mark tells us.

The Gospels abound with such accounts. Jesus who came into the world to save the lost, was likewise Jesus the great physician, the calmer of storms, the provider of human needs—the compassionate Christ. And He left us that example.

Samaritan's Purse has at its core the object and goal of *winning men and women to Christ*. People who are lost, who are dead in sins, break the heart of God. Bob Pierce's commitment and vow before God was to let his heart be broken by the things that break the heart of God.

We, in our generation, would make no less a commitment. If sometimes, as happened to Dr. Bob, fellow Christians do not quite understand or approve our methods, we'll keep on loving them, even if they raise their eyebrows and say, "You call *that* missions?"

13. Tributes to a Good Samaritan

DR. BOB PIERCE WOULD have been the last person to expect or look for the praise of men, or official recognition for his efforts to help people. Nevertheless his compassionate work did not go unrecognized.

During the more than thirty years Bob Pierce served the Lord in foreign countries, again and again he was honored. Royalty, presidents, and other dignitaries presented him with tangible tokens of their appreciation for his tireless work on behalf of widows, orphans, and other suffering people in their countries.

He was three-time recipient of Korea's highest award given to a foreigner and the only man ever to receive the award three times.

Nor were Bob's fellow Americans unaware of his dedicated and tireless service for the needy in Asian countries.

For his work on behalf of China's leprosy victims and orphans, and for shooting and producing the first Christian film—*China Challenge*—Northwestern College in Minneapolis honored Bob Pierce with the degree of Litt.D. (At that same convocation, when Dr. Billy Graham was president of Northwestern, the Governor of Minnesota, Luther Youngdahl, was also awarded a doctorate.)

Actually the photos of Dr. Bob with citations, medals, and other honors would fill a gallery.

But, as people sought to praise him for his service to God and mankind, he would say: "All the accolades of men will be forgotten; they are already forgotten in my life. I have had far more than I deserve, and although lovingly given, they are worthless. There isn't anything of the praise of men that has any value today—only what will bring glory to Jesus is worth striving for, until that day when we gather together at His feet and just praise and worship Him."

Not only during his lifetime, but at his death, Dr. Bob was honored. From around the world, letters poured into Samaritan's Purse office.

Missionaries wrote of their sadness at his homegoing, even while they rejoiced for Bob himself.

Nationals from many lands, whose lives Dr. Bob had touched and blessed, wrote their condolences.

Mission Agencies, for whom time and time again Dr. Bob had put himself on the line to meet a critical need, were quick to voice both their grief at his death and their deep appreciation for his ministry among them. No more fitting tribute could have been paid than that sent by Charles Bennett, president of Mission Aviation Fellowship (MAF), a specialized ministry to remote, isolated mission areas. MAF planes and helicopters, manned by the most intrepid pilots are literally the lifeline— the only link between a jungle missionary and the outside world. On innumerable instances, lives have been saved because MAF came to the rescue.

I would like to share with you Charles Bennett's letter to Samaritan's Purse:

> The message we sent to the family of our beloved Dr. Bob is equally applicable to you who have worked so closely together with him in recent years:
>
> *In loving memory of one who had courage to challenge, faith to expect, and determination to accomplish. Our lives are richer, our horizons broader, for having known Dr. Bob.*
>
> I first came in contact with Dr. Bob during the Korean war. I was a student at Moody Bible Institute. He spoke and showed his

films in Chicago's Orchestra Hall. I was deeply moved and challenged.

I did not see him again until he came by my office about four years ago. As you know, our contacts since then have been frequent and his impact on Mission Aviation Fellowship has been great. Far greater than the mere provision of new aircraft. He truly did broaden our horizons in many ways.

I must confess that I was skeptical when Dr. Bob told me he felt God wanted to provide ten aircraft for MAF through Samaritan's Purse. I considered three or four a more realistic goal. His second plane was an expensive twin, followed shortly by a more expensive jet helicopter and the still more expensive "Nomad." When I suggested that he should perhaps stick to single-engine Cessnas if he wished to reach his goal of ten, he merely laughed.

But he *did* reach ten. And he was talking of number eleven shortly before his death.

On behalf of the MAF Board of Directors, our missionaries scattered around the globe and our people in Kalimantan and Irian Jaya in particular, thank you for your part in providing the structure which allowed Dr. Bob Pierce to exercise his very unique gifts. Our lives and the lives of thousands of "little" people around the world are richer because of the influence of Dr. Bob.

Our prayers are with you as you seek God's will for Samaritan's Purse for the future.

Very cordially in Christ,

Charles Bennett
President

World Vision magazine, in an article titled "Humanity's Friend" (Oct. 1978 edition), published letters of tribute to Dr. Pierce, founder and longtime president of World Vision—an organization for ministry to the world's needy. With their gracious permission we are including some of them in this book.

How different the world would be today if the Christian church had been doing over the last 100 years what Bob Pierce led us to in the most recent 25 years. Bob . . . led the Body of Christ to a more biblical compassion for the truly desperate of the globe. In allowing his heart to be broken time and again, he was used of God to bring physical and spiritual healing to untold numbers of the world community. . . .

It has been said that a true leader is "one who has a gap between himself and the status quo." People who were with Bob on the far-flung missions reflect upon his amazing gift of discernment that allowed him, even under enormous pressure, to await the clear leading of the Lord before critical decisions were made. There is no question that a number of countries are different today because of the life and ministry of this faithful servant who waited on God with a broken heart.

> Mark O. Hatfield
> United States Senator

Dr. Pierce was a man of faith and love. . . . He preached Christ wherever he went, and he helped people physically and mate-rially. . . . He was a friend of orphans, widows, refugees, and all the poor. . . . The people of Korea can never forget him, for he was the best-known preacher of the gospel and welfare worker from abroad during the Korean War. . . . God be praised for him.

> Kyung Chik Han
> Pastor Emeritus
> Young-Nak Presbyterian Church
> Seoul, Korea

(Pastor Kyung Chik Han flew to Los Angeles and preached at his beloved friend's funeral.)

> Lover of God and men,
> Servant of Christ and others,
> Evangelist,
> Humanitarian,
> World statesman—
> All of these, and much more
> Dr. Bob Pierce was to me.

In the early days of World Vision, we enjoyed a very deep and intimate relationship that was profoundly meaningful to me. There is no way to measure or express my personal gratitude to God for the friendship of Dr. Pierce and for the many ways in which my ministry was influenced by him as a model.

His homegoing is a great loss to the world, but I am sure his entry was gloriously triumphant.

> Richard C. Halverson, Pastor
> Fourth Presbyterian Church
> Washington, D.C.

(Dr. Halverson presently serves as Chaplain of the United States Senate.)

Thank you, Bob. Thank you for your example of practical compassion which God used to change and redirect my own life. Thank you for being a "doer of the word" and not a hearer (or talker) only. . . . Thank you for the example of your transparent openness—your rugged honesty about yourself, your relationship with God and with others. Please know that you will always be a part of my life and this work. . .and part of the service of many others whom God has touched through you. Thank you, Bob.

> Larry Ward, President
> Food for the Hungry

Whenever we faced a crisis, Bob was always there to help. Because of his vision and passionate faith that God would provide, we pushed out into areas of need we would never have dared without his encouragement. The words of a Robert Frost poem, which he once asked me for, reflected so well his own spirit:

> The woods are lovely, dark and deep.
> But I have promises to keep,
> And miles to go before I sleep.
> And miles to go before I sleep.

Speaking for hundreds of missionaries around the world who loved Dr. Bob, who depended upon him, who loved to see him come, I can freely say that there was no one as dearly beloved.

> Lillian Dickson
> Mustard Seed, Inc.

A Canadian Remembrance

Dr. Bob Pierce made an unforgettable impact on the conscience of Canadians in regard to suffering, hunger, privation and the misery of war during the decades of the 50s and 60s. By means of radio and his intimate personal letters, he vividly portrayed the aftermath of the Korean War and the plight of homeless orphan children.

His outreach to the people of Vietnam in the throes of Civil War, and his appeal for wheelchairs for the amputee victims of that war aroused Canadians to share and give as they had not done since the days of World War II.

Bob's first public meeting in Canada was held in Brantford, Ontario in the Fall of 1952. From then on as time and energy permitted, he loved to speak and share his personal films with concerned people across Canada.

The results of his ministry in Canada carry through even to the present as Canadians to a major degree continue to contribute to the cause of missions and to the relief of suffering and privation in the Third World.

To all who knew Bob Pierce he was the personification of Christian compassion.

> Robert N. Thompson
> Former Member of Parliament
> Founding Chairman of World Vision Canada
> Vice President, Samaritan's Purse of Canada

All the foregoing loving, sincere words of commendation were really for those whom Dr. Bob left behind; those who loved him and mourned his passing. For Dr. Bob himself was reserved the reward of the faithful laborer who has laid down his tools and stands in the very presence of the Lord he loved and served: "Well done, good and faithful servant; . . . enter thou into the joy of thy Lord" (Matt. 25:23, KJV).

Post Script

As you have been reading this book you might have wondered about its title and how we derived it. Recently I was speaking on the phone with Rev. Roy Gustafson, a man who has had an impact on my life equal to that of Bob Pierce. In our conversation he quoted James 1:8, "A double-minded man is unstable in all his ways" (KJV). Then he said, "How often we have heard of one who 'is a jack-of-all-trades, and master of none.' This could never have been said of the Apostle Paul, who declared: 'this one thing I do' (Phil. 3:13). There was one great compelling drive in his life.

"The same could be said of Bob Pierce. Bob did one thing all of his life, and that was to lead people to the foot of the Cross where they would put their faith in a risen Lord Jesus Christ."

Bob Pierce was a man who wholly committed himself to God, and he firmly believed that when God burdened his heart with a deep need he was not to rest until he had done something about it—regardless the cost. He was truly "single-minded" in his commitment to Christ. It was important to Dr. Bob that the readers of this book understand his commitment. So it's appropriate that *Dr. Bob himself* should have the last word.

By the time you read this, I'll be in heaven.

So many things make me yearn to get on home before the last of the night shades have fallen. It's getting along about sundown, and I must soon hurry to the tool shed and put away my hoe and shovel

216

and all the little implements of the past. There is no sadness in that last walk to the tool shed when you are walking from there into the warmth and light and love of the hearth and home and all the things that the soul most deeply longs for.

I want to remind people that when you're coming close to death and you haven't any other strength, if you belong to Jesus, you can breathe in this strength which is His strength. As long as there are two brain cells that can get together and agree in prayer to trust God, you can believe that He will give you strength. "As your days, so shall your strength be" (Deut. 33:25, RSV).

I want to testify that my whole life is a story of God rewarding faith, and overcoming my flaws, and overcoming my ignorance, and overcoming my resentment of discipline, and in the end overcoming every suffering with His glory and His triumph.

All the stories that are in this book of how God brought us to the point of trial and the unendurable and the insufferable and the intolerable just prove that God was God and in the end triumphed. Faith did win and the compensations were not imitation; they were real. I'm not dying a poor man.

I might have lived the kind of life where the millions stuck to my hands, but I made a commitment to God in the first months of the Korean War that, if He'd trust me with the money to take care of ten thousand children for ten years, I would never let a cent of it stick to my hands.

I suppose at the end of my life now, I can't really say that I have any regrets. And, one of the sweet things about Jesus is that, the nearer you get to heaven, so many things that you ought to be ashamed of, the Blood has already so cleansed that they don't harass you. There is peace. What if the Lord let the mountain of all your sins become so unbearable that it would kill you? But somehow, in His loving way, he doesn't.

I can tell you that, when you are just outside heaven, all that matters is that you loved and served Jesus, that you have not "blushed to speak His name" or compromised for anything that might substitute for the pure gospel.

Many dear friends want me to ask God for more time, but I don't want to live another second beyond His time for me. We all know people who lived one day too long and undid so much. I don't want that.

On my deathbed in the City of Hope, I have one message only. I don't care what you have attempted, what you have succeeded at, or what has been your work in Christ's Name while you are here on earth—only one thing matters when you have reached the last step before you go to stand before Christ:

Did you tell men and women who Jesus is?

Did you bring them to some comprehension of His redeeming love?

Did you make it plain to them that He alone can pay their way to heaven through His atoning death on the cross?

When—and it will be soon—I stand in the presence of a Holy God who knows all there is to know about Bob Pierce, I want to have done all that, standing before His face, I'll wish I had done. When I remember all the opportunities He gave me and the grace He made available, I want to be able to rejoice that I gave Him all the glory.

We are all just a heartbeat from deathless death. *Today, Lord, we look at death not as a friend, but as an enemy, but Jesus is bigger than death, and someday we shall have bodies to match our spirits. Praise the living God! Father, I thank you for all who have been so helpful down through the years. Lord, I want to thank You for these wonderful, wonderful hours with friends. So, Lord, help us to see Thy glory in the days to come more than we have ever seen it before.*

I want those of you who are reading this to know that at this moment the blood of Jesus cleanses. Hallelujah! Jesus is so glorious. Heaven is so real; you just can't know how real heaven is. The glory of all of it is that, with all my sins and blunders, I never turned away from the certain knowledge that I was to bring men to Jesus Christ. Everything I ever did that helped a leper or an orphan or a widow—the sole, only purpose was not that they might have a better life, but that they might have *eternal life* by the experience of salvation through Jesus Christ, our Lord.

By His grace and for His glory, *this one thing* I have strived to do while He gave me breath; as Paul wrote in Philippians 3:

. . . this one thing I do, forgetting those things which are behind, and reaching forth unto those things which are before, I
press toward the mark for the prize of the high calling of God in
Christ Jesus (vv. 13, 14, KJV).

—BOB PIERCE

ROBERT WILLARD PIERCE

1914–1978

Robert Willard Pierce was born in the state of Iowa on October 8, 1914, of humble godly parents. Converted at an early age he heard God's call to serve Him, and until his death in The City of Hope Medical Center in California on September 6, 1978, the overriding passion of his life was to obey that call, whatever the cost. The "call" he translated into the tireless meeting of both spiritual and human need.

A natural communicator, Dr. Pierce studied for the ministry at Pasadena Nazarene College in California.

Married to a pastor's daughter, Lorraine Johnson, he was the proud father of daughters Sharon, Marilee, and Robin.

Prominent in Youth for Christ in its beginning days, founder and president of World Vision, founder of Samaritan's Purse, "Dr. Bob" will long be remembered (perhaps best) for his Korean Orphan Choir who sang their way into hearts around the world.

His work in producing the first Christian films earned him the Litt. D. degree from Northwestern College in Minneapolis.

Innumerable honors came his way from grateful government leaders and heads of state for his Christ-like compassion-in-action. The president of Korea presented him not once, but three times with the highest honor Korea can bestow upon a foreigner. On his deathbed (preparing for yet another trip) Bob Pierce's prayer was still, "Let my heart be broken with the things that break the heart of God."